BORDERS, CITIZENSHIP, AND PREGNANCY

Global Migration and Social Change

Series Editors: **Nando Sigona**, University of Birmingham, UK and **Alexandra Délano Alonso**, The New School, US

This series showcases original research that looks at the nexus between migration, citizenship, and social change. The series aims to open up interdisciplinary terrain and to develop new scholarship in migration and refugee studies that is theoretically insightful and innovative, empirically rich, and policy engaged.

Also available in the series:

Find out more at:

bristoluniversitypress.co.uk/
global-migration-and-social-change

BORDERS, CITIZENSHIP, AND PREGNANCY

Migrant Women's Experiences of Pregnancy and Maternity Care in the UK

Gwyneth Lonergan

First published in Great Britain in 2025 by

Bristol University Press
University of Bristol
1–9 Old Park Hill
Bristol
BS2 8BB
UK
t: +44 (0)117 374 6645
e: bup-info@bristol.ac.uk

Details of international sales and distribution partners are available at bristoluniversitypress.co.uk

British Library Cataloguing in Publication Data
A catalogue record for this book is available from the British Library

ISBN 978-1-5292-3451-0 paperback
ISBN 978-1-5292-3453-4 ePub
ISBN 978-1-5292-3452-7 OA PDF

Cover design: Andrew Corbett
Front cover image: Stocksy/Liliya Rodnikova
Bristol University Press uses environmentally responsible print partners.
Printed and bound in Great Britain by CPI Group (UK) Ltd, Croydon, CR0 4YY

Bristol University Press' authorised representative in the European Union is:
Easy Access System Europe, Mustamäe tee 50, 10621 Tallinn, Estonia,
Email: gpsr.requests@easproject.com

For James and Eva

Contents

Series Editors' Preface:
Bordering and the (Re)production of the 'Ideal Birthing Citizen'

Nando Sigona and Alexandra Délano Alonso

In *Borders, Citizenship, and Pregnancy*, Gwyneth Lonergan examines how migrant women navigate pregnancy and maternity in an environment shaped by restrictive immigration policies and systemic inequalities.

By centring the voices and experiences of migrant women, Lonergan offers an essential critique of how the governance of reproduction and citizenship are mutually constitutive, revealing the profound impacts of policy, discourse, and practice on intimate aspects of life.

Drawing on fine-grained narratives and rigorous analysis, *Borders, Citizenship, and Pregnancy* explores how state-led bordering processes infiltrate maternity care and other systems of social support, disciplining and stratifying reproduction. These processes, deeply racialized, gendered, and classed, construct an 'ideal birthing citizen' – a figure who embodies neoliberal expectations of autonomy, economic productivity, and 'responsible' reproductive behaviour. Migrant women who do not conform to this ideal often face systemic exclusion, substandard care, and even outright harm. Yet, this book is also a testament to the resilience and resistance of migrants who navigate these challenges to assert their dignity, rights, and autonomy.

A key contribution of this book is its application of a reproductive justice framework, which moves beyond narrow notions of 'choice' in maternity care. Lonergan highlights how the ideal of 'patient choice' often masks deeper inequities, framing 'good' choices in ways that align with societal expectations of sacrifice and self-sufficiency while ignoring the systemic barriers that constrain true autonomy. Through this lens, the book critiques how bordering processes and institutional practices deny many migrant women the conditions necessary for genuine reproductive freedom. It joins longstanding calls for a broader understanding of reproductive justice as a human right that encompasses bodily autonomy and equitable access to care for all, regardless of immigration status, race, or socioeconomic position.

Lonergan's work underscores the mutually constitutive relationship between reproduction and citizenship. As the book demonstrates, policies and discourses around reproduction mediate migrants' access to rights, resources, and recognition. This stratification of reproductive rights and responsibilities reveals the state's role in defining who is 'worthy' of belonging and whose reproductive practices align with national ideals.

Bordering processes proliferate across multiple sites of social life, including housing, income support, and healthcare. These processes interact in complex ways, reinforcing systemic exclusions while occasionally opening spaces for resistance and mediation. The result is a highly stratified landscape of reproduction, where access to care and support is uneven and contingent on one's perceived 'deservingness'.

We are delighted to add Lonergan's book to the Global Migration and Social Change series. The book is not only a critical academic intervention but also a call to action to address the systemic inequalities faced by migrant women, including the abolition of immigration controls that stratify reproductive rights, the provision of free and accessible maternity care for all, and the adoption of policies that prioritize reproductive justice over bordering practices.

13 December 2024

Glossary

<table>
<tr><td>BRP</td><td>Biometric Residence Permit, which confirms the holder's immigration status and entitlements while in the UK. At the time of writing, it is being phased out in favour of e-visas.</td></tr>
<tr><td>Clinical Commissioning Groups</td><td>Replaced Primary Care Trusts under the Health and Social Care Act 2012, taking over commissioning responsibilities. Comprised of GP practices with 'advice from a range of other healthcare professionals' (The Health Foundation, 2024d).</td></tr>
<tr><td>Coalition government</td><td>When no party won an overall majority of seats in the House of Commons in the 2010 national election, the Conservative party, who had the most seats, and the Liberal Democrats formed a coalition government under Prime Minister David Cameron (Conservative) and Deputy Prime Minister Nick Clegg (Liberal Democrat). They remained in power until the 2015 national election.</td></tr>
<tr><td>Conservative government (2015–2024)</td><td>Between 2015 and 2024, the Conservative party were the ruling party of the UK, through successive national elections (2015; 2017; 2019). There were multiple Prime Ministers through this period: David Cameron (2015–2016); Theresa May (2016–2019); Boris Johnson (2019–2022); Liz Truss (2022); and Rishi Sunak (2022–2024). The Conservative party held a majority of seats in the House of Commons throughout, except between 2017 and 2019, when no party held an overall majority.</td></tr>
<tr><td>District Health Authorities</td><td>Established in 1982 across different locales in England to 'assess local health needs, employ staff and plan and</td></tr>
</table>

administer hospital and community services' (The Health Foundation, 2024a).

Equality Impact Assessment

Required by the Equality Act 2010 to ensure that the law does not discriminate against individuals on the grounds of age, disability, gender reassignment, marriage and civil partnership, pregnancy and maternity, race, religion or belief, or sex or sexual orientation (Department of Health, 2013a).

Friendly Society

A co-operative contributory insurance scheme; important providers of health insurance in the UK prior to the establishment of the NHS.

International Health Surcharge

Fee added to family, work, and student visas ostensibly to defray the costs of migrants on these visas to the NHS.

***Jus soli* citizenship**

Legal principle whereby anyone born on the soil of a country is automatically a citizen of that country (as opposed to *jus sanguinis* citizenship, where citizenship is determined by parentage, regardless of place of birth).

New Labour government

Between 1997 and 2010, the Labour party were the majority party in the UK House of Commons, under Prime Minister Tony Blair (1997–2007) and then Prime Minister Gordon Brown (2007–2010). They were referred to as 'New Labour' to reflect the decision taken by the party in 2015 to revoke Clause 4 of its founding constitution calling for nationalization of key British industries (Rodrigues, 2015).

NHS

National Health Service – the publicly funded, single payer healthcare system of the UK. Properly speaking, the NHS is actually made up of four national health systems, as the governments of Wales, Scotland, and Northern Ireland each have jurisdiction over their own national system, while control of the English NHS is held by the Westminster government (Bevan et al, 2014).

NHS Trust

Legal entity responsible for providing healthcare goods and services (NHS England, 2024). One or more hospitals are often grouped together in a trust for the provision of secondary care.

Overseas Visitors Officers	NHS staff responsible for determining eligibility for free secondary care.
Primary Care Trusts	Established by the Health Act 1999 to take over commissioning responsibilities from GPs and health authorities (The Health Foundation, 2024b).
Un(der) documented migrant	Refers to a migrant who is in a country without an official visa status and/or without the means to prove their immigration status.

Acknowledgements

I have been very fortunate to benefit from the support and advice of many, many people and institutions in developing and carrying out the research on which this book is based, and in writing the book itself. First, this project was funded by the Wellcome Trust, grant number 209915/Z/17/Z. In addition to the funding, the feedback I was given during the application and interview process was invaluable in the development of this research project.

The original idea for this project grew out of my PhD research on migrant women's activism in Manchester and Sheffield, which was supervised by Bridget Byrne and Jonathan Darling at the University of Manchester. Both Bridget and Jonathan helped me in developing the ideas and questions underpinning this project. Thanks also to Hannah Lewis, Louise Waite, and Emma Tomalin, from whom I learned a great deal as a research associate at the University of Sheffield.

This project was carried out as a postdoctoral fellow at Lancaster University, and would not have been possible without the amazing and supportive intellectual community I found there. I am especially grateful to Imogen Tyler for her tireless support and guidance in developing and undertaking this research; I do not think this book would exist without her. Thank you to all my colleagues in the Department of Sociology, the Migrancy Research Group, ReproNorth, and the Doctors Within Borders network, especially Michaela Benson, Giovanni Bettini, Karen Broadhurst, Erica Consterdine, Rachael Eastham, Jasmine Fledderjohann, Karolina Follis, Tracey Jensen, Corinne May-Chahal, Sayaka Mikoshiba, Lisa Morris, Ala Sirriyeh, Fran Stephenson, and Elena Zambelli. Special thanks to Anne-Marie Fortier for her ongoing mentorship.

I am also grateful to have found a wonderful community of scholars at Northumbria University. Thanks to all of my colleagues in the Department of Social Sciences, especially my fellow members, past and present, of the Sociology team: Sarah Bowman, Mark Cieslik, Ned Coleman-Fountain, Ekaterina Gladkova, Carly Guest, Darryl Humble, Jana Kujundzic, Orla Murray, Charlotte Nisbet, Seema Patel, Sarah Ralph-Lane, Nathan Stephens-Griffin, Carol Stephenson, Paul Stretesky, and Alison Wilde; and especially my co-directors of the Power and Intersecting Inequalities Research group: Nafhesa Ali, Caroline Burns, and Aarti Ratna. Special thanks are due to Ruth Lewis for guiding me through my first two years at Northumbria. I am also very grateful to Kathryn Cassidy for her support and guidance in writing this book.

I have benefitted immensely from the advice and support of a wider community of friends, scholars, and activists, including Gabriella Alberti, Leah Bassel, Esme Cleall, Erin Cullen, Umut Erel, Bethan Harries, Maggie O'Neill, Mary Partington, Tracey Reynolds, Lisa Riedner, Alice Robson, Laura Schwartz, Kate Smith, the sisters and comrades of Feminist Fightback, and my wonderful colleagues in Social Scientists Against The Hostile Environment and the City of Sanctuary Maternity Stream Research Network. Particular thanks to Laura Sochas for reading an early draft of Chapter 5. In addition, findings from this project have been presented at multiple workshops and conferences, and I am grateful to the other participants for their insightful questions and feedback; one such question by Rishita Nandagiri shaped parts of the conclusion of this book. Thank you also to Nando Sigona, Anna Richardson, and Emily Ross at Bristol University Press for their advice and guidance.

There are not the words to express my gratitude to everyone who agreed to be interviewed for this project. I am also grateful to the many organizations who shared information about my project and put me in touch with research participants. I am choosing not to name them in order to preserve the anonymity of my interviewees, but I hope they know that their support was very much appreciated. My thanks also goes to everyone who worked as an interpreter on this project: Nawal Ali, Fatima Bouhaffs, Nacera Harkati, Sarah Ogbay, Tayeba Safeer, and Mitslal Tesfay. This research could not have been carried out without your work, and I appreciate the grace with which you navigated the extra challenges posed by the COVID-19 pandemic.

I am very grateful for the love, patience, and support of my family in Canada and the UK: my mother-in-law Val Stephenson; my parents Peter and Eileen; my brother Liam, sister-in-law Liza, and their children; my sister Katie and her partner Brendan; and most of all my husband James and daughter Eva. This book could not have been written without James' emotional, intellectual, and practical support especially, and words are insufficient to express my gratitude and my awareness of how fortunate I am to have you.

1

Introduction

On 15 May 2023, the British Conservative MP Miriam Cates delivered a speech at the National Conservatism Conference in London decrying declining birth rates in the UK as 'the most pressing issue of our generation' (Cates, 2013). Cates blamed the declining birth rates on 'cultural Marxism' – an antisemitic dog whistle – and called for a reduction in immigration as part of the solution. She also suggested that it is women who are responsible for raising children and that the devaluing of motherhood (rather than parenthood) had contributed to the decline. While Cates stopped short of explicitly suggesting that it is white British women who should have more babies,[1] other politicians associated with National Conservatism have been less circumspect. Giorgia Meloni, the Prime Minister of Italy, has introduced a raft of policies to encourage Italians to have more children and has also previously endorsed 'great replacement theory', which holds that there is a conspiracy (usually involving Jewish people) to replace white Europeans with racially minoritized migrants (Vohra, 2023). In this view, white Europeans need to have more babies, while the fertility of (racially minoritized) migrants poses a direct threat to the nation state.

Although most politicians are not as explicit as Meloni, anxieties around the reproductive practices of migrant women, and what they mean for the future of the nation state, are not new, nor are they confined to the far right. There is an existing body of scholarship discussing how anxieties around reproduction have historically informed, and continue to inform, immigration policies and bordering processes across the Global North (Klug, 1989; Yuval-Davis et al, 2005; Gedalof, 2007; Luibhéid, 2013; Erel, 2018; Siddiqui, 2021). Nonetheless, I believe we are at a particular moment of crisis with regard to the relationship between reproduction and citizenship, with significant implications for the reproductive autonomy of migrants. The far right is resurgent and increasingly normalized across Europe, and indeed, the world (Mondon and Winter, 2020), with migrant fertility and reproduction one of its key concerns (Erel, 2018; Siddiqui, 2021). There is an ongoing attack on reproductive rights more broadly, as exemplified by the striking

1

down of *Roe v Wade* in the US.[2] Additionally, neoliberal restructuring has resulted, in many places, in significant state retrenchment from support for biological and social reproduction (Feminist Fightback, 2011; Bhattacharyya, 2015). Finally, there is an intensification and proliferation of bordering processes, extending the reach of the state in the reproductive lives of both migrants and citizens (Cassidy, 2018; Lonergan, 2018; 2024b; Yuval-Davis et al, 2019; Sahraoui, 2020b; Cassidy et al, 2023).

This book explores migrant women's experiences of pregnancy and maternity care in the north of England, and what they reveal about the relationship between reproduction, citizenship, and bordering processes at this juncture. Reproduction and citizenship are fundamentally intertwined and mutually constitutive. For the survival of the nation state, citizens must reproduce themselves, both biologically, by having children, and socially and culturally, by raising those children and inculcating them with the values of 'good' citizenship. The state therefore has an investment in shaping, disciplining, and regulating reproduction in order to secure that national future. Discourses, policies, and practices around citizenship differentially distribute social, cultural, and material support for reproduction and reproductive autonomy according to hierarchical and multi-tiered constructions of belonging. At the same time, discourses and practices around reproduction, which themselves are gendered, raced, and informed by neoliberalism, structure the national future and shape policies, practices, and experiences of citizenship. Citizenship shapes and disciplines reproduction, but reproduction also emerges as a key axis interacting with and reconfiguring citizenship, at both the individual and the social scales.

Bordering processes – the dynamic, contingent policies, practices, and discourses that govern entry and settlement into a country – both reflect and reinforce discourses around citizenship and belonging, determining who can be a citizen and on what terms. The perceived ability of migrants to reproduce the nation state 'correctly' informs who is seen as a 'desirable' future citizen (Yuval-Davis et al, 2005; Luibhéid, 2013), and discourses around reproduction are a key element in the production of an individual's social location with regard to immigration policies. Bordering processes additionally dictate the level of state support for the reproductive practices of different immigrant groups, determine who is able to live with their family, and even determine what constitutes a 'proper' family (Bonizzoni, 2011; Wray, 2011; Turner, 2020). In recent years, the proliferation and intensification of bordering processes into the spaces of everyday life (Yuval-Davis et al, 2018; 2019) has extended and strengthened the reach of the state in disciplining the reproductive practices of migrants. However, it has also opened up new paths for undermining, and resisting, this disciplining, as bordering processes encounter, and potentially clash with, the philosophies and practices specific to different bordering sites.

The relationship between citizenship and reproduction, and the way this is materially experienced by migrants, is especially visible in maternity care provision. Maternity care is rarely explored through the lens of citizenship, and research that does explore this tends to focus on either statutory access to state health services (see Pařízková et al, 2024) or discourses around health citizenship that call on pregnant individuals to 'manage' the risks associated with pregnancy and childbirth (see Kennedy and Kodate, 2015; McPhail et al, 2016). While both topics are important, and explored in this book, I contend that citizenship shapes debates around what constitutes 'good' maternity care, as well as how maternity care is organized and delivered. Maternity services are the literal site of the biological reproduction of the nation state, and norms and practices around maternity care are informed by narratives around what constitutes 'good' motherhood, which mothers can be trusted to reproduce the nation, and what society 'owes' birthing mothers. This book posits the existence of an 'ideal birthing citizen' constructed through maternity care policy and practice in the UK, which both reflects and reinforces the wider relationship between citizenship and reproduction. Depending on their social location, migrants may be excluded, partially or fully, from this construct, affecting their experience of maternity care and causing them to be subjected to reproductive injustice. Proliferating bordering processes can cause or compound this exclusion, preventing migrants from behaving as the 'ideal birthing citizen'.

Existing literature in the fields of public health and midwifery in the Global North indicate that migrant women are under-served by existing maternity services, and some migrant women are significantly more likely to have poor maternal outcomes. However, there is relatively little scholarship analyzing these findings in relation to citizenship and bordering processes (but see Phillimore, 2015; 2016; Feldman, 2021; Nellums et al, 2021). Migrant women are a diverse group, with a range of national, ethnic, and class backgrounds, and differing levels of education and access to resources, all of which will affect their experience of pregnancy and their maternal health. Existing research suggests that, in high-income countries, the extent to which migrant women are at a higher risk for maternal mortality and morbidity varies (Pedersen et al, 2014; Eslier et al, 2023). In the UK, migrant women, as a group, are not more likely to die in childbirth than British women (Bunch and Knight, 2023);[3] however, there is significant evidence that racially minoritized migrant women, as well as asylum seekers, refugees, and un(der)documented women, do have disproportionately high levels of maternal mortality and morbidity (Jayaweera and Quigley, 2010; Heslehurst et al, 2018; Nellums et al, 2021; Walker and Farrington, 2021). In the UK and other high-income countries, migrant women are more likely to book their first antenatal appointment late and attend fewer antenatal appointments over the course of their pregnancy (Phillimore, 2015; 2016; Heslehurst et al, 2018; Higginbottom et al, 2019; Zhu, 2023; Pařízková et al, 2024). Other barriers to adequate care include: difficulties navigating unfamiliar maternity services (Small et al, 2014; Aquino et al, 2015; Higginbottom et al, 2019; Fair et al, 2020); language barriers (Aquino et al, 2015; Phillimore, 2015; 2016; Fair et al, 2020; Obionu et al, 2023; Sudhinaraset et al, 2023); poor communication with, and insufficient information from, healthcare professionals (Small et al, 2014; Aquino et al, 2015; Fair et al, 2020; Obionu et al, 2023); financial costs of attending appointments (Phillimore, 2015; 2016; Shortall et al, 2015; Heslehurst et al, 2018; Higginbottom et al, 2019; Fair et al, 2020); and a multitude of stressors related to family, work, and immigration status such that women de-prioritize antenatal care (Phillimore, 2015; 2016; Heslehurst et al, 2018; Fair et al, 2020; Nellums et al, 2021). With regard to the UK specifically, the policy of charging un(der)documented migrants for maternity care has been linked to at least three maternal deaths between 2015 and 2017 (Knight et al, 2019), and is acknowledged to have a deterrent effect on seeking out timely antenatal care (Feldman, 2017; 2021; Nellums et al, 2021; Obionu et al, 2023). Furthermore, while some migrant women report having positive experiences of NHS maternity services, multiple studies also found that pregnant migrants were subjected to culturally insensitive and disrespectful care (Aquino et al, 2015; Higginbottom et al, 2019; Obionu et al, 2023).

In the rest of this chapter, I will outline the theoretical framework of this book, starting with a discussion of the concepts of reproductive justice and stratified reproduction, the key analytical lenses through which I explore migrant women's experiences of pregnancy and maternity care. I then elaborate on how this book conceptualizes citizenship and bordering processes, and their relationship to reproduction. This is followed by an account of the fieldwork I conducted with migrant women, NHS staff, and third sector workers in Manchester, Leeds, and Kirklees, the choices I made around methodology, and how all of this was impacted by the Covid pandemic. I finish this chapter with a brief plan of the rest of the book.

Before beginning, however, a brief discussion regarding terminology is necessary. In both discourses around reproduction, and government policy, it is (cisgender) women who are constructed as the people who get pregnant and have babies, and are responsible for raising those babies. Additionally, all the migrant parents interviewed for this project were cisgender women (as far as they disclosed to me). This book therefore largely speaks of 'women' as responsible for biological reproduction and as the group experiencing pregnancy and maternity care. In reality, though, some people who get pregnant and give birth are non-binary people or transgender men. There are therefore points in this book where I refer to birthing people, especially when speaking generically of pregnancy and childbirth, and not about gendered discourses around reproduction or the specific experiences of my participants. Trans and non-binary pregnant migrants and migrant parents will face the obstacles to reproductive autonomy discussed throughout this book, compounded by transphobia. It is not my intention to erase these experiences, and further research is required on this topic.

Second, the UK is made up of four nations – England, Wales, Scotland, and Northern Ireland – each with their own governments. Immigration and citizenship policy are under the jurisdiction of the UK Parliament in Westminster; therefore, I will usually write about UK and British policies and discourses around citizenship and bordering processes. Responsibility for healthcare provision, however, is devolved, so that the parliaments of Wales, Scotland, and Northern Ireland are responsible for the NHS in those nations, while Westminster retains power over the English NHS (Bevan et al, 2014). Therefore, when discussing NHS policy and practices as it affected my participants, I am writing about the NHS in England, and English policy. Further complicating this, as I outline in Chapter 2, the NHS figures prominently in the British national imaginary and understandings of British identity. I have attempted to be as precise as possible when discussing policies and discourses as they relate to different nations and levels of government. It is beyond the remit of this book to consider how discourses around national belonging and the NHS, and the lived reality of these discourses and policies, are mediated by Scottish, Welsh, and Northern Irish identities, and I offer my sincerest apologies to readers from these nations who feel that this book does not do justice to their experiences.

Reproductive justice and stratified reproduction

Reproduction

This book primarily locates pregnancy and childbirth within the wider set of discourses, practices, and processes that constitute reproduction. Reproduction can be understood as encompassing both biological reproduction and social reproduction, that is, 'the various kinds of work – mental, manual, and emotional – aimed at providing the historically and socially, as well as biologically, defined care necessary to maintain existing life and to reproduce the next generation' (Laslett and Brenner, 1989: 383; see also Yuval-Davis, 1997; Erel, 2018).

Social reproduction includes all the tasks involved not only in raising children, but in raising them to be members of a particular society, and inculcating them with appropriate values and behaviours. This is a broader definition than that traditionally used by Marxists, who understand social reproduction as the reproduction of the working class and the class structure of society (Laslett and Brenner, 1989). However, social reproduction can also be defined more expansively as encompassing the reproduction, across generations, of the population, as well as wider social structures and inequalities, including gender, racism, and class. Thus, Erel (2018: 174), drawing on Fraser (2016), posits 'reproduction as an activity that reproduces humans as social and cultural beings while at the same time reproducing the cultural, social and economic structures, including inequalities.'

Additionally, it is critical to recognize that social reproduction informs biological reproduction. Ideas around what constitutes a 'good' pregnancy and birth are socially constructed, and informed by wider discourses around 'good' mothering (Lowe, 2016; Hooberman et al, 2023). This is explored in more detail in Chapter 5.

Reproductive justice

The US-based Women of Color Reproductive Justice Collective, Sister Song (n.d.), defines reproductive justice as 'the human right to maintain personal bodily autonomy, have children, not have children, and parent the children we have in safe and sustainable communities'. The framework was first developed by African American feminists in their analysis of, and response to, struggles around reproductive health in the US, and based on conversations with feminists and women's rights activists from the Global South at the 1996 UN Conference on Population and Development in Cairo (Ross, 2006; Bond Leonard, 2017). However, there is a long history of racially minoritized women, in the US as well as in the UK and other countries, arguing for the necessity of a broader, critical perspective on reproductive 'choice' (Combahee River Collective, 1977/1981; Davis, 1981; Bryan et al, 2018; Samantrai, 2002; Ross, 2006).

The reproductive justice framework places reproductive activities and decision-making within the wider material and discursive context in which they occur, a context shaped by intersecting systems of oppression, including racism, patriarchy, capitalism, ableism, homophobia, and transphobia. The material and social resources necessary for genuine reproductive autonomy are differentially distributed according to patterns produced by these intersecting systems of oppression, and according to discourses that construct certain individuals and groups as 'good parents' and 'valued members of society' and others as threatening (Solinger, 2001; Ross, 2006; Davis, 2009; Roberts, 2017; Ross et al, 2017). The reproductive justice framework casts a wide net, exploring how interacting discourses, polices, and institutions – including, for example, welfare state policies (Solinger, 2001; Roberts, 2017), the judicial system (Roberts, 2017), maternity care provision (Davis, 2019a; 2019b), and immigration policies (Lonergan, 2012; Abji and Larios, 2021) – constrain reproductive activities and decision-making. In doing so, the framework problematizes the liberal, individualist approach of the mainstream pro-choice movement, arguing that the absence of legal barriers to contraception and abortion is insufficient for genuine reproductive autonomy (Davis, 2009; Roberts, 2017; Ross et al, 2017); as Dorothy Roberts (2017: 308) argues, 'the abstract freedom to choose is of meagre value without meaningful options from which to choose and the ability to effectuate one's choice'. The reproductive justice framework thus draws our attention to, and facilitates analysis of, the multiple interacting factors shaping the relationship between citizenship and reproduction and the resulting constraints on migrants' reproductive autonomy.

Stratified reproduction

Stratified reproduction provides a framework for analyzing how reproduction and reproductive tasks are 'differentially experienced, valued, and rewarded according to inequalities of access to material and social resources in particular historical and cultural contexts' (Colen, 1995: 78). The concept, first developed by Shellee Colen (1995), examines how the state and other social institutions provide different levels of support for individual and collective reproductive tasks, reflecting wider patterns of social divisions and inequalities (see also Ginsburg and Rapp, 1995; Castañeda, 2008; Bonizzoni, 2011; Wu et al, 2019). Strikingly, this may involve state and social support for individuals and groups to care for other people's children but not their own; the experience of migrant childcare workers forced by economic necessity and immigration controls to live apart from their own children is a key topic in studies of stratified reproduction (Colen, 1995; Smietana et al, 2018). While, as noted earlier, stratified reproduction was originally used to analyze differential support for reproduction, scholars have expanded this focus to encompass differential support for reproductive autonomy more broadly (see also Ginsburg and Rapp, 1995; Humphris, 2017; Solazzo, 2019; Moniz et al, 2022).

Stratified reproduction is an intersectional framework, as scholars use it to explore the ways in which multiple, interacting, social structures and institutions, including capitalism, racism, and gender, as well as state policies operating at different scales and in different contexts, serve to stratify support for reproduction and reproductive autonomy (Colen, 1995; Ginsburg and Rapp, 1995; Beynon-Jones, 2013; Smietana et al, 2018). This is combined with a granular analysis, which investigates how stratified support for reproduction both shapes and is mitigated by the particular situation and circumstances of individuals (Mamo and Alston-Stepnitz, 2015; Lonergan, 2024a). Finally, research around stratified reproduction may also consider how the views and actions of people providing reproductive healthcare may be shaped by wider discourses that differentially value the reproductive activities and autonomy of different individuals and groups, and the material consequences (Goldade, 2011; Beynon-Jones, 2013). This is particularly salient to this book, as proliferating border controls have both co-opted medical professionals into the implementation of bordering practices (Cassidy, 2018) and provided professionals with new opportunities to contest or undermine these processes.

There is a great deal of overlap between reproductive justice and stratified reproduction, as both frameworks are interested in how support for reproduction, and reproductive autonomy, is differentially distributed by the state and wider social institutions. There are, however, important differences, which is why both are deployed in this book; there are times when the reproductive justice lens is more suitable, and others when stratified reproduction provides a sharper and more productive analysis. Smietana et al (2018: 117) note that reproductive justice emerged out of an activist milieu, and suggest that 'stratified reproduction is primarily an analytic and descriptive concept whereas reproductive justice names both an activist movement and an analytic framework'. They later add: 'Stratified reproduction is mostly about relative resource poverty and socioeconomic gradients that fuel working class labour migration. Reproductive justice is more concerned with reproductive abjection, societal discrimination, and state institutions that use race as a technology to tear apart rather than support some kinds of families.' (117)

Building on this, I find that reproductive justice provides a more radical, structural critique that is not only interested in uneven patterns of resource distribution, but how these relate to wider discourses around identity and belonging, and the reproductive future of a society, which makes it particularly useful when conceptualizing the relationship between reproduction and citizenship. Stratified reproduction, on the other hand, provides a granular analysis of how the differential distribution of resources is experienced materially in the daily lives of individuals. It is especially helpful in considering the lived experiences of my participants in their full complexity, shaped as these are by the complicated, contingent relationship between citizenship and reproduction and the foreclosures and new possibilities created by proliferating bordering processes. In the next section, I further develop the theoretical framework of this book by outlining how citizenship, and the relationship between citizenship and reproduction, is conceptualized.

Citizenship

Citizenship can be broadly defined as the rights and responsibilities associated with membership in a political community (Purcell, 2003; Benhabib, 2004), usually the nation state.[4] It is useful to distinguish between formal citizenship, which refers to legal membership in a political community, and substantive citizenship, which encompasses the meaning of citizenship, constructions of identity and belonging, and the lived experience of the associated rights and responsibilities (Holston, 1999; Glenn, 2011). Following Marshall (1950/2009: 148–149), the rights of citizenship can be divided into three categories: civil rights, 'the rights necessary for individual freedom'; political rights, those rights associated with '[participation] in the exercise of political power'; and social rights, more nebulously described by Marshall as 'the whole range from the right to a modicum of economic welfare and security to the right to share to the full in the social heritage and to live the life of a civilised being according to the standards prevailing in the society'. Marshall (1950/2009) understood the social rights of citizenship, or social citizenship (see Dwyer, 2010), as associated with the development of the welfare state, including the NHS. Discourses around national identity and belonging both underpin and mediate policies governing the rights and responsibilities of citizenship (Werbner and Yuval-Davis, 1999; Glenn, 2011). Citizenship should be understood as hierarchical and multi-tiered, with individuals enjoying different 'levels' and 'kinds' of membership depending on their location with regard to these discourses (Werbner and Yuval-Davis, 1999). Individuals and groups may have different rights and responsibilities depending upon how they are constructed within discourses around citizenship; moreover, these discourses serve to produce a continuum of exclusion/inclusion, in which some individuals are seen as 'belonging' more than others. All this shapes the lived reality of citizenship, including access to its entitlements.

In many countries, including the UK, gender is critical to the construction of citizenship. Liberal citizenship is founded on a public/private gendered dichotomy in which the political 'public' sphere is coded as the domain of men and the apolitical 'private' sphere, on which the public sphere depends for coherence, is coded as the domain of women (Pateman, 1989; Lister, 2003). Women were thus initially constructed as 'non-citizens' within liberal discourses of citizenship and their reproductive activities within the home as outside the domain of citizenship. The implications of this will be discussed in more detail later. Discourses around citizenship and belonging are also often intertwined with race and/or ethnicity (Werbner and Yuval-Davis, 1999; Bassel and Emejulu, 2017; Erel, 2018). British citizenship is heavily racialized, associated with whiteness (Gilroy, 1987; Runnymede Trust, 2000; Clarke, 2021). Discussing the British Nationality Act 1981, Tyler (2010) argues that British citizenship is a biopolitics 'designed to fail' racially minoritized residents of the UK. Prior to the Act, Commonwealth citizens settled in the UK were entitled to British citizenship. In combination with immigration policies that privileged white Commonwealth migrants with British ancestry, the Act produced racialized Commonwealth migrants as a 'foreign' population within the UK, both ideologically and, sometimes, legally (see also El-Enany, 2020; Medien, 2021). At present, even as there may be recognition of the UK as an ethnically diverse society, '[w]hiteness itself – as a set of relational ideas and codes – remains fundamental to how Britishness is imagined' (Clarke, 2021: 290). This may be especially true of 'Englishness' (Byrne, 2006), of relevance to this book as the research sites (to be discussed later) were all in the north of England. This racialization of British identity is both reflected and reinforced by immigration policies, elaborated upon in the section on bordering processes.

Additionally, neoliberal restructuring has reconfigured discourses around, and the lived experience of, citizenship in the UK and elsewhere, particularly with regard to social citizenship (Rose, 1999; Nyers, 2004; Brown, 2015). Neoliberalism, which in the UK began to be implemented under the Thatcher government of the 1980s, can be defined as the ideology that the economic wealth of society will be maximized through liberating the market from state interference (Brenner and Theodore, 2002).[5] This includes the 'interference' of a social safety net, such that neoliberalism is characterized by severe welfare state retrenchment. Concurrently, the belief in the efficiency of the market means that remaining state services may be outsourced to private companies (Brenner and Theodore, 2002). Neoliberalism is thus associated with a significant reduction in the entitlements of social citizenship and changes to how the remaining entitlements may be delivered. Furthermore, Brown (2005; 2015) argues that neoliberalism involves the expansion of market logics into other areas of human life. In keeping with this, the implementation of neoliberal economic restructuring has been accompanied by a shift in the understanding of citizenship, with the responsibilities of citizenship emphasized at the expense of the rights (Rose, 1999; Bussemaker, 2005). The 'ideal' neoliberal citizen is independent, autonomous, self-regulating, entrepreneurial, and financially productive (Rose, 1999; Nyers, 2004; van Houdt et al, 2011). Access to what remains of social citizenship may be conditional on demonstrating these qualities (Rose, 1999; Bussemaker, 2005). Gendered, racialized, and neoliberal discourses around citizenship and belonging interact with and inform each other; as I outline in the following section, neoliberalism has specifically reconfigured the rights and responsibilities of citizenship specific to women.

Citizenship and reproduction

Turner (2008: 53) developed the concept of 'reproductive citizenship' as encompassing those rights that address the question 'with whom may one reproduce and under what social and legal conditions?', which, he specifies, includes the right to *not* reproduce (see also Richardson and Turner, 2001; Roseneil et al, 2013; Larios, 2023). This book builds on Turner's (2008) critical work to propose a more expansive view of reproductive citizenship, as incorporating an analysis of the ways in which reproduction informs citizenship. The future of the nation state depends upon citizens reproducing themselves, not only biologically, but socially, inculcating future generations with the values of citizenship. The state consequently has an investment in disciplining and regulating reproduction. Discourses and policies around citizenship contribute to the construction of some individuals as more capable of reproducing the nation state 'correctly' than others, and influence reproduction through the differential distribution of legal rights, resources, and support. Citizenship thus emerges as a key driver of reproductive injustice and stratified reproduction. At the same time, discourses, policies, and practices around reproduction contribute to the construction of citizenship as hierarchical and multi-tiered, and produce individuals into different locations with regard to citizenship, informing their attendant rights and responsibilities, and their experience of citizenship. In short, reproduction and citizenship are mutually constitutive.

Both historically and at present, women have been constructed as responsible for the biological and social reproduction of the nation state (Yuval-Davis, 1997; Erel, 2011). This gives rise to an important paradox with regard to liberal citizenship (Erel, 2011). As noted earlier, liberalism is premised on a gendered dichotomy in which women's reproductive activities within the home are constructed as apolitical and thus as a private matter for which they should expect neither recognition as citizens nor state support (Pateman, 1989). However, these reproductive activities are also crucial to the future of the nation state and are therefore constructed as a legitimate site of state intervention. Thus, women are constructed within discourses around citizenship as responsible for reproduction, and their reproductive activities, and the paradoxical situation of reproduction within liberalism, profoundly shape women's experience of citizenship. Discussing the FEMCIT project researching the impact of women's movements across Europe on gendered citizenship, for example, Roseneil et al (2013: 902) observed that 'the relationship between citizenship and reproduction emerged as a matter of central concern in each of the sub-projects, and thus as part and parcel of the study of each dimension of citizenship'.

The influence of reproduction, and anxieties around reproduction, on women's construction within, and experience of, citizenship is further mediated by their location within wider racialized, classed, and ableist discourses of identity and belonging. Certain women are constructed as more capable of reproducing the nation state 'correctly' than others. At the same time, these women tend to be 'higher' within hierarchies of citizenship and consequently may be seen as more entitled to both civil liberties, including bodily autonomy, and to welfare state services. Somewhat ironically then, the women who are more likely to receive state support for raising children are also more likely to be supported, or at least respected, in their choice to refrain from having children (Solinger, 2001). By contrast, women who are seen as less capable of reproducing the nation state, because of their race, class, disability, and/or immigration status, also tend to be more marginalized within hierarchies of citizenship. Their reproductive practices may consequently be subject to intense surveillance and disciplining by the state, and/or be significantly devalued and unsupported, and they may also be seen as less entitled to reproductive autonomy in general (Solinger, 2001).

In the UK, the association between Britishness and whiteness means that reproductive citizenship is heavily racialized. Racism shapes women's experiences of reproduction, and anxieties around reproduction inform racially minoritized women's construction within, and experience of, citizenship. Tyler (2010) notes that the Nationality Act 1981 abolished *jus soli* citizenship in the UK, such that only babies born in the UK to citizens and those with indefinite leave to remain are automatically entitled to citizenship. Consequently, maternity wards are now literally a site at which 'foreigners' enter the UK (Tyler, 2010). Within the wider context of the Act, which strengthened the racialization of British citizenship as white, this serves to construct racially minoritized mothers, not only as 'foreign', but as introducing a further 'foreign' element in the UK by having babies. Similarly, as I discuss in more detail in Chapter 5, racialized anxieties around reproduction contribute to the erosion of Black women's entitlement to decent healthcare, a key right of social citizenship; as a consequence, Black women are four times as likely to die in childbirth than their white counterparts (Knight et al, 2023).

Reproduction and social citizenship

The mutually constitutive relationship between citizenship and reproduction is particularly visible with regard to social citizenship. The policies, services, and resources associated with social citizenship are critical to both biological and social reproduction, to safe(r) pregnancies and childbirth and to raising children; these include, among others, state-subsidized healthcare provision; social housing provision and regulation of the private housing sector; labour rights, including those associated with parental rights; and state-subsidized childcare (or lack thereof). At the same time, the structure and mode of distribution of these entitlements both reinforces and is underpinned by gendered, racialized, and classed discourses around who should be carrying out reproductive tasks, and how. The British post-war Keynesian welfare state was based on the heteronormative nuclear family model, with a male breadwinner and a female responsible for reproducing the household (Pateman, 1989; Lister, 2003; Bhattacharyya, 2015; Roseneil et al, 2020). To quote Carol Pateman (1989: 192), it was 'presupposed that certain aspects of welfare could and should continue to be provided by women (wives) at home, and not primarily through public provision' (see also Bhattacharyya,

2015). Consequently, in the 1960s and 1970s, the UK government did not subsidize childcare, such that there was an economic incentive for one parent to give up full-time paid work to care for children. The wage gap and traditional gender roles meant that this parent was likely to be the mother. In Denmark, by contrast, concerns about labour shortages in the mid-1960s led to a significant increase in public childcare to encourage mothers into the labour market, at least part-time. Reproductive tasks, however, continued to be seen as 'women's responsibility', thus binding women closer to the welfare state (Borchorst and Siim, 1987). In both contexts, then, welfare state policy not only reflected gendered assumptions around women's role in society, but also served to discipline women into performing this role, shaping their experience of citizenship in other areas (Sassoon, 1987; Bhattacharyya, 2015).

With the advent of neoliberal restructuring, the expectation that households should be financially autonomous, and the lack of economic value placed on reproductive labour, has reconfigured women's rights and responsibilities regarding citizenship, further variegated by class. On the one hand, the expectation that citizens be financially autonomous and economically productive means that women are now expected to engage in paid labour outside the home (Roseneil et al, 2020; De Benedictis, 2012). This is reflected in British welfare policy: prior to 2008, lone parents (disproportionately women) were entitled to income support from the state, enabling them to stay at home with their children until the youngest turned 16; at present, lone parents are expected to look for paid work once their child is three. On the other hand, women are still constructed as responsible for reproduction, a responsibility that has grown more onerous as neoliberal restructuring has involved withdrawal of state support for reproduction (Feminist Fightback, 2011; Bhattacharyya, 2015; Bassel and Emejulu, 2017). Racially minoritized women may be especially impacted by this. The UK welfare state was always racialized; Cohen (1985) discusses how antisemitic immigration controls were used to limit Jewish residents' access to proto-welfare state services pre-World War 2, and anxieties around racialized Commonwealth migrants posing a 'burden' on the welfare state were critical to anti-immigrant rhetoric in the 1950s and 1960s (Samantrai, 2002; Solomos, 2003). Bassel and Emejulu (2017) consequently argue that racially minoritized women's experience of economic precarity is of long-standing, but that nonetheless, these women have been disproportionately harmed by neoliberal restructuring, particularly the imposition of austerity measures.

Responsible reproductive citizenship

Furthermore, the neoliberal emphasis on personal responsibility extends to an expectation that women will reproduce 'responsibly'. Carroll and Kroløkke (2018: 994) coined the term 'responsible reproductive citizenship' to denote how women in the US are called upon to 'risk-manage their reproductive future' by freezing their eggs, 'manag[ing] their present fertility to ensure future fertility'. I wish to expand the term to encompass the multiple ways in which women are expected to take personal responsibility for ensuring that the nation state is reproduced 'correctly'. This includes ensuring that future citizens are self-actualizing, economically productive, neoliberal citizens. Riley and Chatterjee (2023: 147), for example, contend that neoliberal restructuring in Egypt involved women being encouraged to 'contribute positively to the future of the nation' by having fewer children and using contraception. As I argue in Chapter 5 especially, responsible reproductive citizenship entails making 'good choices' with regard to maternity care (see also Lowe, 2016). In the UK, responsible reproductive citizenship additionally associates being in paid work with 'good mothering'; De Benedictis (2012) argues that, under the Coalition[6] government, single mothers who were not in paid work were recoded as irresponsible, 'bad' parents. It also involves demonstrating that one can reproduce without financial support from the state. At the time of writing, parents in receipt of universal credit[7] are only able to claim child benefit on their first two children (Gov.uk, 2021).[8] This can be read as the state engaging in reproductive coercion, leveraging families' reliance on benefits to dissuade them from having more than two children.[9] The policy also sends the message that children born to families on benefits are not 'valued' and that one should not expect to enjoy full reproductive autonomy if one relies upon state support.

Bordering processes

This book understands border processes as a series of dynamic, contingent set of 'practices and discourses that "spread" into the whole of society' (Paasi, 1999: 670 cited in Mezzadra and Neilson, 2013: 13), governing entry and settlement. These processes are not limited to the territorial space of the physical border, but have expanded both within and outside the legal boundaries of the nation state (Mezzadra and Neilson, 2013; Yuval-Davis et al, 2018; 2019). Critically, the purpose of these bordering processes is not necessarily to exclude migrants from the territory of the nation state, although that is certainly an effect of these processes for some migrants. Instead, bordering processes serve as instruments of differential inclusion (Andrijasevic, 2009; Mezzadra and Neilson, 2013), producing different migrants into different legal categories with specific relationships to the state, and as part of this, to the welfare state and the job market. As Mezzadra and Neilson (2013) point out, inclusion and exclusion should be understood as existing along a continuum. Moreover, inclusion may be violent and exploitative, for example, when und(er)documented migrants are 'included' in the economy as an easily exploitable reserve army of labour (De Genova, 2010a; Mezzadra and Neilson, 2013).

Because bordering processes determine who can (and cannot) be a citizen, and on what terms, they reflect and reinforce discourses around citizenship and belonging. Like citizenship, bordering processes are hierarchical and multi-tiered, and consequently one may be included/ excluded to different degrees along multiple axes. Furthermore, the sorting and categorizing function of these processes serves to discipline both migrants and citizens. The conditions attached to entry and settlement associated with different categories indicates which migrants are seen as more 'desirable' and which traits are valued in migrants, thereby producing particular behaviours. Limiting migrants' access to benefits, for example, means that migrants are required to demonstrate economic self-sufficiency to qualify for settlement, reflecting neoliberal discourses around citizenship. Additionally, because migrants are often required to act as 'super citizens' (Anderson, 2013), these conditions also denote what is expected of citizens.

Bordering processes have historically been, and continue to be, gendered, often underpinned by an understanding of the 'typical' migrant as male (Kofman, 2004; Raghuram, 2004; Mahler and Pessar, 2006). As I discuss in more detail in Chapter 3, UK immigration policy conceived of women primarily as dependents of male relatives and consequently restricted, and at times, abolished, migrant husbands' entitlement to join their wives in the UK (Samantrai, 2002; Wray, 2011). Bordering processes also reflect the racialization of citizenship, as noted earlier. Looking specifically at the UK, the Nationality Act 1948 created two categories of British subject: Citizens of the UK and Colonies, and Commonwealth Citizens, both of whom were entitled to enter and settle in the UK at will (Samantrai, 2002; Solomos, 2003). However, successive Immigration Acts throughout the 1960s and 1970s targeted Commonwealth migrants from former colonies in the Global South, stripping them of the entitlements of citizenship, while leaving paths to settlement open to white migrants from the 'Old Commonwealth' (Samantrai, 2002; Solomos, 2003; Small and Solomos, 2006). This culminated, as discussed, in the Nationality Act 1981, which abolished the category of Commonwealth Citizen and further strengthened the association between Britishness and whiteness (Tyler, 2010; El-Enany, 2020). Gender played an important role in the construction of racially minoritized Commonwealth migrants as posing a cultural threat to the UK, necessitating stricter immigration controls. Analyzing the public discourse around the Immigration Acts of the 1960s and 1970s, Samantrai (2002: 64) notes that 'promiscuous sexuality, high rates of birth, arranged marriage, the "traditional" oppression of women, and so forth' were used 'to define alien ways of living'.

The emergence of neoliberal discourses of citizenship had a significant effect on immigration policy and bordering processes within the UK. While previous governments had considered (racially minoritized) immigration to be inherently undesirable, New Labour (1997–2010) adopted a 'managed migration' paradigm, under which migrants who displayed the neoliberal qualities of economic productivity, entrepreneurialism, and self-sufficiency were seen as beneficial to the country. The purpose of bordering processes was consequently to sort migrants according to this criteria and discipline them into displaying these characteristics once in the UK. Thus, the New Labour government introduced the points-based immigration system for migrants wishing to work or study in the UK, in which applicants were judged according to, among other criteria, their previous and potential future earnings (Home Office, 2006). They also initiated the No Recourse to Public Funds policy, under which migrants on student, family, and work visas were forbidden from accessing non-contributory benefits, thereby requiring them to demonstrate economic self-sufficiency. Although New Labour shifted away from the more explicit racialized focus of previous bordering regimes, various policy documents, as well as statements by prominent New Labour MPs and ministers, used coded language to construct racially minoritized migrants, especially Muslims, as posing an economic, cultural, and, at times, security threat to the UK (Burnett, 2004; Worley, 2005; Kundnani, 2014). The 'community cohesion' paradigm, for example, was developed in the wake of urban disturbances between white and Asian youth in the northern English cities of Bradford, Burnley, and Oldham, in the summer of 2001. The paradigm ignored economic deprivation and racism as causes of the disruption, and instead conflated 'racially minoritized' and 'migrant'; it further suggested that (racially minoritized) migrants had introduced a disruptive level of difference to the UK (Burnett, 2004; Worley, 2005; Fortier, 2010). New Labour were also notably hostile to asylum seekers, banning them from paid work and introducing the policy of dispersal – whereby housing is offered on a no-choice basis and residents can be moved at any time without notice – as well as widespread immigration detention (Bloch, 2000; Bloch and Schuster, 2005). This can be read as caused by the challenge asylum seekers pose to 'managed migration'. Asylum seekers' right to stay in the UK depends not on their potential economic contribution, but whether they meet the criteria laid out in the UN Refugee Convention.

The Coalition (2010–2015) and Conservative (2015–2024) governments further entrenched both neoliberal discourses and policies around bordering, and the racialization of 'undesirable' migrants. The Coalition government introduced a minimum income requirement to sponsor one's spouse, thereby making the right to a family life for families with migrant members dependent upon demonstrating a degree of economic self-sufficiency (see Chapter 3). They also significantly increased visa fees and introduced the

Immigration Health Surcharge (see Chapter 2), such that the ability to earn, and save, a great deal of money has become a key criteria for settlement. Moreover, in 2012, then Home Secretary Theresa May gave an interview in which she promised to create a 'really hostile environment' for 'illegal migration' (Kirkup and Winnett, 2012), and in 2013, the Home Office sent vans emblazoned with the slogan 'In the UK illegally? Go home or face arrest' through ethnically diverse areas of London, thus indicating who was imagined as an 'illegal immigrant' (Jones et al, 2017).

Situated, proliferating, intensifying bordering processes

Over the last several years, bordering processes have multiplied and proliferated away from the territorial border, and into the spaces of everyday life (Paasi, 1999; Mezzadra and Neilson, 2013; Yuval-Davis et al, 2018; 2019). Individuals – migrants and citizens – may now have to demonstrate their legal residence in the UK in order to undertake paid work, access secondary care on the NHS free of charge (see Chapter 2), rent a flat, acquire a UK driving licence, or open a bank account. Concomitantly, this means, for many people, it is now a responsibility of citizenship to check other people's papers (Aliverti, 2015; Yuval-Davis et al, 2018; 2019). These proliferating bordering processes are situated, in that individuals experience bordering differently depending, first, on their social location within intersecting discourses around citizenship and belonging, and second, depending on their role with regard to the specific bordering processes they may encounter, for example, whether they are a landlord or a tenant. Bordering processes are additionally shaped and influenced by the site at which they are located (Yuval-Davis et al, 2018; 2019). There is significant evidence that, reflecting wider discourses around British citizenship, the implementation of these processes is heavily racialized, as gatekeepers check for documentation based on their (racialized) perception of who 'seems' British (Yuval-Davis et al, 2018; 2019; De Noronha, 2022).

Furthermore, bordering processes have also become more intense, as the criteria for settlement has both increased and become stricter, and the timeline to settlement has become longer and involves more state surveillance. In 2003, an individual in the UK on a spousal visa had to wait 2 years before applying for Indefinite Leave to Remain; now, such an individual would have to wait 5 years, reapplying for their visa at the 30-month mark, demonstrate that they meet the minimum household income both at the initial application and the 30-month reapplication, pass the Life in the UK Test, and demonstrate an intermediate understanding of English (Sirriyeh, 2015). Visa fees have also, as noted, increased significantly. In 2003, it cost £155 to apply for Leave to Remain by post; at the time of writing, for applicants within the UK, a 30-month spousal visa costs £1,048 with an additional £2,587.50 for the International Health Surcharge.

Bordering and reproduction

The mutually constitutive relationship between reproduction and citizenship is reflected in bordering processes. Bordering processes, and the construction of different migrants within these processes, are informed by anxieties around reproduction. Simultaneously, bordering processes also serve to discipline migrants' reproductive practices and limit reproductive autonomy. Migrant women may be constructed as 'hyper-fertile', having 'too many children' and thus burdening the welfare state and 'replacing' the 'native' population (Castañeda, 2008; Luibhéid, 2013; Erel, 2018; Lonergan, 2018; Coddington, 2020; Siddiqui, 2021). Castañeda (2008: 343–344), for example, notes the use of the term 'demographic theft' in Germany to describe the supposed threat posed to the nation state by the combination of migrant fertility and low birth rates among the German population. Migrant mothers may also be constructed as introducing an untenable amount of difference through their reproductive practices, by failing to raise their children to be 'good' citizens, by acting as obstacles to their native-born children's integration (Yuval-Davis et al, 2005; Gedalof, 2007; Bassel and Khan, 2021), or simply by having children in their new country of residence (Tyler, 2010; Cisneros, 2013). However, the extent to which migrant women's reproductive practices are seen as potentially threatening depends on how these women are located within gendered, racialized, and neoliberal discourses around citizenship and belonging. Within the UK context, for example, racially minoritized migrant women are especially constructed as posing a threat, both through their supposed hyper-fertility and through anxieties about their ability to raise British children (Yuval-Davis et al, 2005; Gedalof, 2007; Tyler, 2010; Bassel and Emejulu, 2017; Coddington, 2020).

Anxieties around this supposed threat informs bordering processes, and the construction of individual migrants within these processes. Migrant mothers' reproductive practices can be seen as necessitating stricter immigration controls; 'maternity tourism' was a key rationale given for restricting migrants' access to the NHS in debates around the Immigration Act 2014 (Lonergan, 2024b; see also Luibhéid, 2013; Erel 2018). Similarly, racially minoritized women may be constructed as particularly undesirable migrants within discourses around bordering because of their reproductive practices. With regard to Ireland, for example, Luibhéid (2013) discusses how racially minoritized asylum-seeking women became the focus of especial anxiety because they were able to have Irish babies, and thereby secure the right to remain in Ireland.[10] On the other hand, in some circumstances, migrant women who are perceived as potentially able to reproduce the nation state 'correctly' may be seen as desirable migrants, when properly disciplined, as Barton (2020) outlines with regard to pro-natalist immigration policy in France in the late 19th and early 20th centuries. Similarly, Fortier (2021) argues that, among the responsibilities acquired by naturalized citizens – migrants who have 'proven' their worth – is that of producing future British citizens.

Bordering processes also serve to discipline women's reproductive practices, by dictating who can form a family within a country and on what terms (Bonizzoni, 2011; Wray, 2011; Sirriyeh, 2015; Turner, 2020), and by differentially distributing the resources necessary for reproduction, for example, by restricting certain migrants' access to the welfare state (Gedalof, 2007; Bonizzoni, 2011; Humphris, 2017). Migrant women may thus be required to demonstrate economic self-sufficiency, in keeping with neoliberal discourses of citizenship, if they wish to have children in the UK (Lonergan, 2018). The proliferation and intensification of bordering processes has increased the reach of the state and the severity of the policing to which migrant women's reproductive practices are subjected. However, as I discuss throughout this book, especially in Chapter 4, it has also opened new opportunities for resistance, as bordering processes encounter, and are mediated by, the philosophies, cultures, and practices of different bordering sites.

Researching migrant women's experiences of maternity care

The fieldwork for this project was conducted between 2020 and 2022, and involved a critical analysis of policy documents around the Immigration Acts of 2014 and 2016 and UK government health and maternity policy (2010–present), notably the 2016 National Maternity Review (*Better Births*); semi-structured interviews with 41 migrant mothers in Manchester, Leeds, and Kirklees; two focus groups of three women invited from the pool of interviewees; semi-structured interviews with 16 NHS employees in Manchester, Leeds, and Kirklees, whose role involved caring for or interacting with pregnant migrants; and interviews with five individuals who worked in the third sector supporting pregnant migrants and new mothers. Additionally, one in-person workshop and one online workshop were held in June and July 2022, respectively, to share the findings of the project and consider how they might be useful to pregnant migrants and their supporters going forward.

The migrant women participants of this project were from a range of backgrounds and immigration 'categories', in order to permit an exploration of how multiple factors, including immigration status, influence the experience of pregnancy and maternity care in England. I interviewed EU citizens who were able to exercise their treaty rights pre–Brexit; women who had come to the UK on work, family, and student visas, or had accompanied a spouse as a dependent on a visa; asylum seekers and refugees; and one woman who was undocumented. There were participants from five continents, with only Oceania and Antarctica unrepresented. Most participants had come to the UK after 2010, and were living in Greater Manchester, Leeds, or Kirklees when they had a baby. I had planned to only interview women who had arrived in the UK after 2010, but the difficulties of recruiting under Covid (to be discussed later) meant I had to be more flexible in my criteria. Nonetheless, all of the women had come to the UK in late adolescence or as adults and so had not 'grown up' with the NHS.

This project was designed prior to the Covid pandemic, and the pandemic required that I reconfigure the planning and conducting of fieldwork. Plans for ethnographic observation in the waiting rooms of antenatal care centres at hospitals in the fieldwork areas had to be cancelled. The initial recruitment strategy for migrant mothers involved working with migrant support groups and attending their drop-ins, as well as visiting groups and drop-ins supporting new parents, for example, 'stay and play' mornings in places of worship. Unfortunately, all of these drop-ins were suspended during the pandemic. Instead, recruitment was done through migrant support organizations who advertised the project to their members, as well as through social media and word of mouth. The suspension of in-person support groups affected the number of migrant mothers recruited to participate in the project, as well as the make-up of the participant pool; the majority of interviewees recruited had some kind of contact with migrant support organizations.

The added pressures brought by the pandemic also made it more difficult for women who are especially marginalized to participate, both because I was less likely to make contact with them through migrant support organizations and because they did not have the time or capacity to be involved in a research project. I decided to interview individuals who work for third sector organizations supporting pregnant migrants, to ensure the challenges faced by the most marginalized pregnant migrants were included in this project. Covid also made it more difficult to recruit NHS staff, who were overwhelmed by their work responsibilities and therefore could not make time for participation in this research. One potential participant who is a midwife cancelled at the last minute because she had been called into work on her day off to cover for the more than 30 midwives in her area that were off sick. Additionally, most (but not all) of the staff recruited had a particular interest in maternity care for migrants and were therefore not necessarily representative of NHS staff as a whole.

The Covid pandemic also impacted how fieldwork was conducted. All interviews and focus groups were conducted on Microsoft Teams or over the phone, depending on the resources available to the interviewee. There exists a wider literature discussing the advantages and disadvantages of online and telephone interviews as compared to in-person interviews (see Sturges and Hanrahan, 2004; Block and Erskine, 2012; Deakin and Wakefield, 2014; Lo Iacono et al, 2016). While not all scholars agree (see Block and Erskine, 2012; Deakin and Wakefield, 2014), I found it more challenging to develop a connection online or over the phone. While interviewees were generally quite generous in discussing sensitive and difficult topics, it is possible that even more information would have been elicited were face-to-face interviews possible. Similarly, telephone interviews made it impossible for me to pick up on non-verbal cues, and these may also have been less visible over Teams. To address potential ethical issues arising from this, I made sure to check in regularly with interviewees to ensure they were not distressed, reminding them that they could pause or end the interview at any point. Nonetheless, no data could be collected regarding body language, nor could body language and facial expression influence how the interview was conducted. However, there may have been some benefits to remote fieldwork as well. Online and telephone interviews offer greater flexibility around time and location, which may be especially useful to mothers with babies and young children. A few phone interviews were conducted over more than one session, as the interviewee could only speak for a limited period of time on any given day, due to caring and other responsibilities. This would not have been feasible face to face.

Several of the interviews were conducted with the support of an interpreter. Participants were asked if they had a preferred interpreter, but none did. Instead, all interpreters, save one, with whom I had worked extensively before, were recommended by migrant support organizations. The presence of an interpreter, especially in phone interviews, may have affected the 'flow' of the interview, as well as the rapport between myself and the interviewee. While this may have been true with an in-person interview as well, it was likely exacerbated by not being in the same room, or being able to see each other's body language, and so on. However, there were a few interviews where the interpreter and interviewee were previously known to, and already comfortable with, each other, and this may have helped the interview run more smoothly than it otherwise would have done. Critically, language barriers proved to be a very important aspect of some of my participants' experiences of maternity care, and whatever disadvantages may have arisen due to the necessity of using interpreters was far outweighed by the significance of hearing the experiences of women who would have struggled to communicate in English with medical professionals.

It is also useful to address my own positionality. I am a white Canadian who has lived in the UK for almost two decades, first as a student, then on a working holiday permit, then a spousal visa, then with Indefinite

Leave to Remain, and very recently, as a UK citizen. As a migrant I have occupied a somewhat liminal space. As a white, middle-class Canadian, married to a white, middle-class British man, I am significantly privileged within discourses around immigration and within immigration policy. As I have been assured on multiple occasions, when white British people complain about immigrants, they don't mean *me*. My interaction with gatekeepers and with medical professionals has been shaped by my racial, class, and linguistic privilege. On the other hand, as my participants discuss in Chapter 3, the necessity of maintaining my visa status and not falling afoul of the Home Office and its constant changing of rules and regulations has been an ever-present source of stress and moderate inconvenience. Moreover, I am a migrant mother myself, someone who, many years ago, navigated an unfamiliar maternity system during pregnancy and childbirth. Nonetheless, I am aware that many of the women I interviewed, especially those in particularly marginalized situations, would have read me as a white British woman, or near enough, despite the persistence of my Canadian accent. This undoubtedly also affected the interviews, compounding the difficulties already discussed earlier around remote fieldwork.

Researching migration in the north of England

NHS maternity provision varies from region to region: some areas offer continuity of carer (see Chapter 2) while others do not; some have specialist maternity teams for asylum-seeking and refugee women, and some do not. Similarly, different cities and towns have varying levels and kinds of support available to migrant parents. I therefore decided to recruit participants from specific cities (or in the case of Kirklees, a specific metropolitan borough). Greater Manchester, Leeds, and Kirklees were chosen for several reasons. All three areas are in the north of England, which has been particularly impacted by the austerity agenda pursued by the Coalition and Conservative governments, which involved making significant funding cuts to both welfare state services and local government (Bambra and Garthwaite, 2015; Johns, 2020; Marmot et al, 2020). Austerity has had a harmful impact on public health in the north of England (Bambra and Garthwaite, 2015; Marmot et al, 2020) and reduced the resources available to local government and the third sector to support pregnant people and migrants. The experiences of migrants in the north of England also tends to be under-researched in comparison to London.

With regard to the specific characteristics of the fieldwork locations, Manchester and Leeds both have specialist maternity support for asylum-seeking and refugee women while Kirklees does not. All three areas have third sector organizations providing support to precarious migrants, and Leeds is the site of the first City of Sanctuary Maternity Stream, a group providing support, including peer support, for pregnant 'sanctuary seekers' and campaigning to create more inclusive maternity services (Yorkshire and Humber Maternity Stream, 2024). Greater Manchester and Leeds are both urban areas, while Kirklees comprises a combination of one large town (Huddersfield) and some smaller towns and rural areas. Greater Manchester's census briefing reports that its population includes people born in 189 different countries and that 'all of the national identities that were recorded across the whole of England and Wales were also recorded within Greater Manchester' (GMCA Research, 2023: 7). The Combined Authority is more ethnically diverse than the national average; as of the 2021 census, 28.7 per cent of residents were from an ethnic minority group (including 'white people who were not white British'), whereas the average for England is 26.5 per cent (GMCA Research, 2023: 3–4). This is even more pronounced in the city of Manchester, where only 57 per cent of residents identify as white (this would, of course, include white migrants) and just under one third were born outside of the UK (ONS, 2023c). By contrast, 79 per cent of the population of Leeds identifies as white, and 82.2 per cent were born in England (ONS, 2023b). In Kirklees, 73.6 per cent of the population identifies as white and 86 per cent were born in England (ONS, 2023a).

Outline of the book

Chapter 2 discusses the evolution of health citizenship in the UK, especially as it pertains to pregnant and birthing women, and the role of the NHS in demarcating the boundaries of national belonging. I explore how maternity provision for migrants in England has been shaped by twin policy agendas, neoliberal restructuring within the English NHS, and immigration controls restricting access to the NHS. I also identify the existence of an 'ideal birthing citizen' in current NHS policy and practice, a pregnant woman who actively engages with maternity services and who makes 'good choices' regarding her care, both to safeguard her baby's health and to improve NHS services. This chapter provides additional theoretical and policy context for the next three chapters, which present the empirical findings from my fieldwork. Chapter 3 looks at the role of family bordering processes in structuring my participants' experiences of reproduction, including pregnancy, maternity care, and new motherhood. Because the (heteronormative nuclear) family is constructed as the 'legitimate' site for the reproduction of the nation state, family bordering processes are informed by anxieties around reproduction and serve to shape and discipline the reproductive practices of families with migrant members. They determine who can be a family and on what terms, and reflect and reinforce the state recognition of certain family forms (but not others). The disciplining of family forms also serves to discipline reproductive practices, differentially distributing access to state and family support for pregnant migrants and indicating who is considered a 'proper' citizen that can be trusted to reproduce the nation state. Chapter 4 then explores the bordering of social citizenship, including NHS bordering, as an instrument of stratified reproduction, especially as regards maternity services. What emerges is a highly variegated portrait of reproductive stratification, as multiple bordering processes overlap and interact with each other to provide differential access to NHS maternity services, further refined by the situations of individual women and the resources available to them. This stratified reproduction is additionally complicated by the interaction of bordering processes with the professional commitments and practices of some midwives, who emerge as a key source of support for pregnant migrants in negotiating restrictive immigration policies. Chapter 5 explores my participants' experiences of maternity care, arguing that there is an 'ideal birthing citizen' constructed through maternity policy and practice in England – the person who *should* be reproducing the nation state. In keeping with wider discourses around citizenship and reproduction, she is a white, self-actualizing neoliberal citizen who speaks fluent English, can navigate NHS maternity services, and makes 'good choices' – or risks having them made for her. Pregnant and birthing people may experience reproductive injustice and stratification, and even obstetric violence, where they fail to conform to this ideal. The concluding chapter reiterates the empirical findings of the book, and what they reveal about the relationship between citizenship, bordering processes, and reproduction, and makes suggestions for addressing the stratified reproduction and reproductive injustice faced by birthing migrants in England.

2

Citizenship, Health, and 'Responsible' Reproduction

Introduction

In Chapter 1, I outlined the complex and mutually constitutive relationship between citizenship and reproduction. The future of the nation state depends on the biological and social reproduction of citizens; consequently, discourses and practices around reproduction inform, and are informed by, gendered, racialized, and classed discourses and policies around citizenship and belonging. Policies, services, and resources associated with social citizenship are shaped by anxieties around national reproductive futures. At the same time, these policies differentially distribute services and resources necessary for reproduction, and serve to structure and discipline reproductive practices. The nature, intensity, and experience of state intervention into reproduction depends on how an individual is constructed within hierarchical and multi-tiered discourses around citizenship, and whether she is understood as 'capable' of reproducing the nation state 'correctly'.

A key vector for state intervention into reproduction is through maternity services. As a form of healthcare, state provision of maternity care is a right of social citizenship in many wealthy countries;[1] however, as De Vries et al (2002b: xii) point out, unlike other medical care, '[w]hat is at stake in care at birth is not the survival of one patient but the reproduction of society'. The peculiar status of maternity care as both an entitlement of social citizenship and as critical to the national future means that anxieties regarding the reproduction of the nation state may inform contestations around the rights and responsibilities of citizens as they pertain to this care. Concurrently, these same contestations may influence discourses and practices around maternity care.

This chapter traces the influence of two key sets of discourses and policies around healthcare as a right of social citizenship, how these have been informed by, and inform, notions of reproductive citizenship, and

25

who is capable of reproducing the nation state 'correctly'. In doing so, this chapter outlines important elements of the policy context in which my participants experienced, and made decisions around, pregnancy and maternity care. The first set of discourses and policies relates to NHS bordering – the use of bordering processes to differentially distribute access to NHS healthcare. The NHS enjoys a special position within the British national imaginary, constructed as a uniquely 'British' institution and a source of national pride. As I will explore, it has long been imbricated in the construction of racialized and gendered discourses around belonging and citizenship; however, this role has been strengthened in recent years by the implementation of bordering processes within the NHS. Anxieties around the reproduction of the nation state played a key role in the creation and enactment of these processes, and in the deployment of the NHS in delineating the boundaries of national belonging.

The second set of discourses and policies relate to the neoliberal restructuring of the English NHS, beginning under the Thatcher government and gathering momentum under New Labour and the Coalition governments, and the concurrent emergence of a neoliberal model of 'health citizenship', which constructed 'good health' as the moral responsibility of the individual citizen. Individuals are expected to make 'good choices', not only for their own health, but also to leverage their power as consumers to improve and maintain NHS services. These expectations have informed recent iterations of 'responsible reproductive citizenship' as it pertains to women's engagement with maternity services, and the construction, in maternity policy and practice, of an 'ideal birthing citizen' – the person who *should* be reproducing the nation state.

I begin this chapter by outlining how I understand 'health citizenship', drawing on Jauho and Helén's (2023) definition, which includes policies and discourses around the rights and responsibilities of citizens as they pertain to health and healthcare, as well as how individuals may be differently located within these policies and discourses depending on their 'vital capacities'. The chapter then provides a brief history of the role of the NHS in the delineation of the boundaries of national belonging before engaging in a more in-depth exploration of the implementation of bordering processes within the NHS as part of the Immigration Act 2014, and the specific deployment of the figure of the 'pregnant migrant' in the creation of these processes. I then discuss neoliberal restructuring within the NHS, and the expectation that citizens make 'good choices' to maintain their health and safeguard NHS services. This expectation has informed maternity services and the current iteration of the 'responsible reproductive citizenship', contributing to the emergence of an 'ideal birthing citizen' in policy and practice around NHS maternity services.

Defining health citizenship

This book follows Jauho and Helén (2023) in understanding health citizenship, as encompassing: the rights and responsibilities of citizens as it relates to their health; policies governing access to healthcare; and state interest in the vital capacities and capabilities of individuals and groups (this latter element will be discussed in more detail later). Porter (2011) associates the emergence of health citizenship with the French Revolution, which declared health to be one of the 'rights of man'. Concurrently, citizens were seen as having a responsibility to the nation to maintain their health by adopting good habits. With the development of welfare states in wealthy nations in the 20th century, access to healthcare came to be understood as a key right of social citizenship, and in the decades following World War Two, most wealthy countries (with the notable exception of the US) developed some form of universal healthcare system (Olafsdottir and Bakhtiari, 2015). These systems not only consolidated healthcare as an entitlement of citizenship, and the responsibility of the state, but also became implicated in nation-building discourses and projects, and contributed to defining the territorial and ideological space of the nation state (Bivins, 2015; Kivelä and Moisio, 2017).

Critically, however, citizenship is contested, hierarchical, and multi-tiered (Werbner and Yuval-Davis, 1999). Discourses, policies, and practices around healthcare provision may both reflect and reinforce contested and variegated understandings of citizenship and belonging (Olafsdottir and Bakhtiari, 2015; Kivelä and Moisio, 2017). Healthcare provision may be intertwined with bordering processes; these processes may limit access to healthcare for some categories of non-citizens, and surveillance through the healthcare system may enable the identification and expulsion of undocumented migrants (Olafsdottir and Bakhtiari, 2015). An individual's location within discourses around citizenship and belonging may shape which healthcare services they are entitled to, and the kind of care delivered. Moreover, in recent decades, neoliberal restructuring has transformed the provision of healthcare in the UK and other wealthy nations, as well as understandings of the rights and responsibilities of citizenship around health; in particular, there is increasing emphasis on the expectation that citizens take responsibility for their own health (Crawford, 2006; Brown and Baker, 2012; Cairns and Johnston, 2015).

The 'vital capacities and capabilities' of individuals are an additional factor shaping their location within, and experiences of, discourses and policies around health and health citizenship. Jauho and Helén (2023: 468) define 'vital capacities and capabilities' as those traits that are 'are biologically elementary, crucial for their viability, and often seen as congenital', which would include capabilities associated with pregnancy, childbirth, and childrearing. Incorporating the 'vital capabilities' of individuals into the conceptualization of health citizenship involves exploring how 'biological and medical facts and related expert knowledge enter in and influence the domains in which citizenship is defined and struggled over' (Jauho and Helén, 2023: 469).

Illustrating this, Jauho and Helén (2023) discuss the ways in which the perceived 'vitality' of citizens shapes their rights and responsibilities in Finland; for example, historically people with chronic illnesses were barred from social benefits because they were reserved for citizens deemed capable of supporting themselves financially in the future, while at present, entitlement to compensation for a workplace injury, which is a social right of citizenship, in practice depends upon a medical assessment of the degree of injury (Jauho and Helén, 2023).

A definition of health citizenship that encompasses 'vital capacities' is useful for this book because women's reproductive biology is foregrounded in how they are constructed in discourses and policies around citizenship, as responsible for reproducing the nation state. Furthermore, the rights and responsibilities of women's social citizenship as they relate to reproductive health are shaped by debates around what constitutes 'good' maternity care, which are in turn underpinned by contestations around women's reproductive capacities, for example, how much medical intervention in pregnancy and childbirth is 'ideal'. Critically, 'expert opinion' regarding maternity care and women's vital capacities may be racialized, classed, and ableist, such that birthing people receive different kinds of care and experience healthcare differently, depending on their location within discourses of citizenship and belonging. Debates around 'good maternity care', and the rights and responsibilities of mothers, are discussed in more detail in Chapter 5.

The NHS and the gendered and racialized boundaries of health citizenship

The UK NHS came into existence on 5 July 1948 (Greengross et al, 1999). It replaced a piecemeal system of healthcare provision combining private services; health insurance provided through trade unions and friendly societies; contributory health insurance run through the state for workers who did not earn enough money to participate in trade union or friendly society schemes; and charity hospitals. Many people were not able to access medical care consistently, especially women, as many of the above schemes required members to be in paid work (Jones, 1994). The NHS, through which the state guaranteed access to medical care free of charge for all citizens, marked a pivotal turning point in health citizenship in the UK, and was a key aspect of the creation of a post-war welfare state that transformed social citizenship (Thane, 1996; Olafsdottir and Bakhtiari, 2015). The establishment of the NHS was an acknowledgement that social citizenship encompassed the right to healthcare; moreover, the NHS itself became central to gendered and racialized discourses around what it meant to be British (Bivins, 2015). Furthermore, as Bivins (2015: 13) argues, the NHS, and associated public health campaigns, represented 'more than a national commitment to health equity', becoming 'a prized symbol of Britain's national status and modernity'. The NHS continues to enjoy a unique place within the British national imaginary, treated as one of the country's greatest successes and a symbol of British identity. The opening ceremony of the 2012 Olympics in London included a ballet about the NHS; politicians routinely refer to 'our NHS'; and it is possible to buy t-shirts and tote bags emblazoned with the slogan 'Born in the NHS'. This last example points to the imbrication of the NHS not only with British national identity, but the reproduction of the nation state. The slogan itself is a play on the lyrics of the Bruce Springsteen (1984) song 'Born in the USA'. In that song, the phrase 'born in the USA' serves as an assertion of citizenship, because the US has *jus soli* citizenship – to be born in the USA is to be an American citizen. To be born in the NHS, then, is similarly treated as a marker of Britishness, which, as I discuss later, contributes to the construction of pregnant migrants and their non-citizen babies as posing a threat to not only the NHS, but the UK as a whole (see also Lonergan, 2024b).

Immigration, the NHS, and the racialized nation state

From its inception, the NHS was imbricated in struggles around who could be British, and on what terms. Initially, the NHS was free at the point of delivery to anyone, regardless of immigration or citizenship status; however, the National Health Service Act 1949 empowered the Minister of Health to make regulations that charged anyone deemed not 'ordinarily resident' in the UK for NHS services (Cohen, 1985; Cassidy, 2018; Medien, 2021). While, as I discuss later, such regulations were not introduced until 1982 (Medien, 2021; 2023), and not actually implemented until 2006, the fact that the possibility of doing so was introduced so soon after the creation of the NHS is striking. The NHS became intertwined in bordering processes and discourses around citizenship in other ways. Following World War Two, citizens of UK colonies and the Commonwealth were allowed to enter and settle in the UK at will; this was envisaged as both addressing the post-war labour shortage and strengthening ties within the wider empire as decolonization began. However, racially minoritized migrants from current and former colonies were the subjects of significant anxiety around both their impact on the welfare state and the possibility that they would settle permanently (Samantrai, 2002; Solomos, 2003; El-Enany, 2020) (see Chapter 1). These dynamics were very much present within discourses and policies around the NHS and health citizenship more broadly. Racially minoritized migrants filled important positions within the NHS, as doctors, nurses, porters, cleaners, and so on, but were also portrayed as a burden on the NHS and as bringing disease to the UK (Bivins, 2015). Additionally, from the 1960s onwards, struggles around racially minoritized migrants' access to, and impact on, the NHS were occurring within a wider context of increasingly restrictive, racialized immigration controls, as outlined in Chapter 1. These immigration controls served to limit the number of racially minoritized migrants who could settle in the UK and make use of the NHS.

Anxieties around the reproductive practices of racially minoritized migrant women were part of these debates around health citizenship and belonging in the nation state. Bivins (2015) argues that it was particularly through their reproductive capacities that racially minoritized women were understood as posing a threat to the British national community. Racialized migrant women were seen, first, as having 'too many' children, and second, as failing to raise 'healthy' children (Klug, 1989; Bivins, 2015). The so-called 'failed maternity' of migrant women, according to Bivins (2015: 10), was 'represented both by genetic and nutritional disorders among their children'. Consequently, racially minoritized pregnant migrants and migrant mothers could be subject to disciplining and surveillance through the NHS, for example, with regard to anti-tuberculosis campaigns (Bivins, 2015). Racially minoritized pregnant migrants were also seen as potentially using the NHS illicitly and/or posing an economic burden; Cohen (1985) cites the example of Leicester General Hospital requiring Asian women attending antenatal clinics to provide proof they were entitled to NHS care, even though such internal controls were, at the time, illegal.

NHS bordering and the reconfiguration of the boundaries of belonging

While the NHS may long have been imbricated with racialized and gendered discourses around belonging and citizenship, in recent years it has become more directly implicated with bordering processes. As mentioned earlier, the National Health Service Act 1949 allowed the Minister of Health to impose charges on patients deemed to be not 'ordinarily resident' in the UK, but it was not until 1981 that the government announced their intention to impose such charges, which came into effect on 1 October 1982 (Medien, 2021; 2023). Critically, these charges were planned within the wider context of the introduction and passage of the British Nationality Act 1981, which, as discussed in Chapter 1, abolished the automatic entitlement to British citizenship of Commonwealth citizens settled in the UK, and strengthened the association between Britishness and whiteness, constructing racialized residents of the UK as 'foreign', discursively, and sometimes, legally (Tyler, 2010; El-Enany, 2020; Medien, 2021). The charges were understood by activists at the time as targeting racialized people living in the UK, depriving them of access to a welfare state service that was seen as 'uniquely British' while also subjecting them to surveillance, and implying that racialized communities were a burden on the welfare state (Medien, 2021; 2023). NHS bordering from its inception, then, was intertwined with wider attempts to redefine the limits of British citizenship and belonging. The charges were ultimately not implemented following sustained campaigning by anti-racist activists (Medien, 2021; 2023).

The NHS and the 'hostile environment'

Charging for NHS secondary care was first introduced in 2006 by the New Labour government, who decided to implement the provisions made in the National Health Service Act 1949 (Cassidy, 2018; Medien, 2021). Patients could be charged for secondary care if they were considered not to be 'ordinarily resident' in the UK, with 'ordinarily resident' understood to mean anyone living in the UK with citizenship or an immigration status that permitted them to stay for 6 months or more (Department of Health, 2013b). However, visa checks to determine eligibility were not mandatory, and were often carried out in an arbitrary and ad hoc manner, varying from hospital to hospital. This changed with the Immigration Act 2014, and associated policy instruments, which further implicated the NHS in bordering processes, as part of the wider 'hostile environment' programme of the Coalition government (see Chapter 1). The NHS became involved in this proliferation of internal bordering processes in two main ways. First, it became mandatory for hospitals to charge eligible patients for secondary care and to carry out visa checks to determine eligibility. A series of financial incentives and sanctions were established to induce hospitals to carry out these checks; NHS trusts are able to charge patients deemed ineligible for free care 150 per cent the cost of the treatment, allowing them to turn a considerable profit at a time when the NHS is in a funding crisis (discussed later). Ineligible patients are expected to pay in advance of receiving care, unless it is deemed by clinicians to be 'urgent and immediately necessary' (Department of Health and Social Care, 2024: 5). This means that clinicians have become embroiled in NHS bordering processes as their assessments determine whether a patient can get care without paying first (Cassidy, 2018). Any outstanding debt to the NHS may be cited by the Home Office as a reason to refuse to regularize a migrant's status or grant them a visa in future (Feldman, 2021). Moreover, from 1 January 2017 to 9 November 2018, there existed a memorandum of understanding between the Home Office and the Department of Health such that the latter provided patient information – including 'a patient's last known address, date of birth, GP's details and the date registered with a GP' (Doctors of the World, 2018: 1) – to the Home

Office for the purposes of immigration enforcement (Home Office and Department of Health, 2017). The NHS thus became directly implicated with the deportation of un(der)documented migrants. The memorandum was withdrawn following a sustained campaign by migrants' rights activists.

Second, the Immigration Act 2014 also introduced the Immigration Health Surcharge (IHS) on family, student, and work visas, ostensibly to defray the costs of the visa holders to the NHS. The charge was initially introduced as £200 per visa per year (£150 for students) (Cassidy, 2018), but this quickly increased; it currently stands at £1,035 per visa per year (£776 for minors or students) (Gov.uk, n.d.–c). Cassidy (2018) argues that NHS bordering can be read as part of a wider project to maximize the economic benefits of migration and tourism, ensuring visitors pay for care and raising more funds through the IHS. This is reflected in consultation documents published by both the Home Office (2013a; 2013b) and the Department of Health (2013b; 2013c), both of which are, initially at least, ambivalent regarding the economic basis for the IHS. On the one hand, there are repeated assertions that non-European Economic Area (EEA) migrants[2] must make a 'fair contribution' to the NHS so as not to be a burden to the UK taxpayer; on the other hand, there is also considerable concern around whether the introduction of the IHS will be economically beneficial or if it will dissuade desirable 'highly skilled' migrants, including students, from moving to the UK (Lonergan, 2024b). Furthermore, the IHS can be read as disciplining migrants into demonstrating economically productive behaviour, in keeping with neoliberal models of citizenship; in order to apply for, or renew, a visa, a migrant must prove they are sufficiently high-earning to save up the increasing sums required. As will be discussed in Chapter 3, escalating visa costs also serve to discipline migrant women's reproductive practices.

Beyond this, the introduction of the IHS additionally served to redefine who could be considered 'at home' in the UK, thereby further tying the NHS to the delineation of the boundaries of national belonging (Lonergan, 2024b). As noted earlier, 'ordinarily resident' for the purposes of accessing the NHS was initially taken to include all migrants on a visa that permitted them to stay in the UK for 6 months or longer. However, in both government documents and Parliamentary discussions around the Immigration Act 2014, it is repeatedly asserted that the non-EEA migrants on work, family, and student visas are, in fact, temporary and therefore not 'at home' in the UK. In explaining the rationale for the IHS, the Home Office's (2013a: 6) call for consultation on the proposal states: 'We are therefore consulting on a proposal to change the existing "ordinary residence" test which governs free access to the NHS to exclude *temporary* non-EEA migrants.'

Indeed, it is suggested in the Department of Health's response to their consultation that the IHS is necessary precisely *because* these migrants are not 'at home', do not have a 'permanent relationship' with the UK, and thus it is only 'fair' that they pay for the NHS: 'For temporary migrants there was also support for seeking a fair contribution towards the cost of their care until they have formed a permanent relationship with the UK.' (Department of Health, 2013c: 13)

The implementation of NHS bordering in the Immigration Act 2014 reflected and reinforced pre-existing racialized discourses around citizenship and belonging. As noted in Chapter 1, the 'illegal immigrant' targeted by the Immigration Act 2014 was racialized in the popular imagination and government discourse as non-white, as exemplified by the infamous 'Go Home' vans incident. Similarly, the Qualitative Research Report (Creative Research, 2013: 29) commissioned by the Department of Health to research the 'impact' of 'temporary non-EEA migrants' on the NHS suggested that such migrants were likely to be found in areas with 'diverse local ethnic populations' (Lonergan, 2024b). It was further suggested that, within these communities, visitors were engaging in 'health tourism' with the support of (non-white) British family members, thus constructing racially minoritized residents with migrant family members as 'less' British and as posing a threat to the NHS: 'There were also anecdotes of family members coming to the UK on annual visits and using the occasion to have a check-up or access treatment' (Creative Research, 2013: 29).

Pregnant migrants and NHS bordering in the Immigration Act 2014

Anxieties around the reproduction of the nation state played a significant role in the creation and implementation of NHS bordering in the Immigration Act 2014. While, as discussed, migrant women's reproductive practices have historically informed how they are constructed within discourses and policies around health citizenship, this took on new salience in the Immigration Act 2014 because of the way in which access to the NHS was deployed in redefining who could be considered 'at home' in the UK. As a result of the introduction of the IHS, pregnant migrants on work, family, and student visas were constructed as 'temporary' and 'not at home' in the UK. This reinforced the concerns about whether these migrants were capable of reproducing the nation state correctly, and limiting their access to NHS maternity services therefore became necessary for disciplining the introduction of a 'foreign population' – their babies – into the country. At the same time, though, by creating a family in the UK, migrant women can be read as asserting that they *are* at home. The introduction of the IHS, and the association between the use of the NHS and being 'at home', may paradoxically serve to strengthen these claims – what could be more British than a baby 'born on the NHS'? Limiting pregnant migrants' access to NHS maternity services thus becomes necessary both to safeguard the national reproductive future and to maintain the use of the NHS in delineating the boundaries of belonging (Lonergan, 2024b).

Unsurprisingly, then, within policy documents and Parliamentary debates, the figure of the racially minoritized pregnant migrant emerged as a key problem to be addressed through NHS bordering (Lonergan, 2024b). The 'maternity tourist' is constructed as justifying the need for stricter controls around access to the NHS. The Home Office's (2013a) original call for consultation on proposed changes to NHS access states, for example: 'Within the NHS, there is considerable anecdotal evidence of abuse, relating to *maternity services* and treatment for acute conditions including cancer and renal services, as well as access to other routine elective procedures.' (22; emphasis added)

Similarly, giving evidence in the public bill committee during Parliamentary debates around the Immigration Act 2014, Jacqueline Bishop, the co-chair of the Overseas Visitors advisory group of the NHS asserted: 'In my hospital, I do not think we have one particular area that people come for. Maternity is rife throughout. Anyone who says that they do not have overseas visitors in maternity either are not doing their job properly or just have their head in the sand.' (Parliament. House of Commons, 2013: 8)

Critically, there is frequent slippage between 'maternity tourist' and 'temporary non-EEA migrant', especially within the Qualitative Research Report (Creative Research, 2013). This suggests that *any* use of NHS maternity services by racially minoritized migrants is illicit and threatening. The report, for example, provides 13 quotes from NHS staff discussing examples of 'visitors who fly in and fly out' (that is, intentional health tourists); five of these quotes involve use of antenatal care – a disproportionate focus on maternity services – and of these, three were about pregnant migrants who would have been considered 'ordinarily resident' in 2013 (Creative Research, 2013: 38–41). Both the Department of Health's (2013c: 29) response to the consultation and the Department of Health's (2013a) Equality Impact Assessment of the Act cite the Qualitative Research Report as providing evidence that 'deliberate maternity health tourism through the short-term visit entry is a problem', endorsing this expansive understanding of 'maternity tourist'. Additionally, reinforcing the racialization of non-EEA 'temporary' migrants, West African pregnant migrants are singled out as posing a burden to NHS maternity services, in both the Qualitative Research Report (Creative Research, 2013) and Parliamentary debates (see Parliament. House of Commons, 2013) (and, indeed, in press coverage of NHS bordering at the time [see Gilligan (2013)]) (Lonergan, 2024b). In short, racially minoritized pregnant migrants, including those with legal entitlements to NHS maternity care, were constructed as especially threatening to the NHS and as justifying further restrictions on access to NHS secondary care for *all* migrants.

Perversely, the construction of pregnant migrants as especially threatening to the NHS, and therefore necessitating stricter bordering, is further consolidated by the acknowledgement that they may be a vulnerable group. Both the Home Office (2013b) and Department of Health (2013a; 2013c) recognize that charging un(der)documented pregnant migrants for care could result in serious harm to some people. Yet, it is suggested that this harm is justified by the supposed cost these migrants pose to the NHS:

> [T]he risks to the health of both the mother and baby if refused or deterred by the need to pay are significant ... However, our independent research confirms that deliberate maternity health tourism through the short-term visit entry is a problem, and this could only increase, potentially significantly, if services were provided free of charge. We therefore shall not be introducing any new exemptions from charging for maternity services. (Department of Health, 2013c: 29)

Importantly, the Department of Health (2013c) estimated the cost of *all* 'health tourism', of which 'maternity tourism' is only one part, to have been between £20 million and £100 million per year in 2013 – or between 0.018 per cent and 0.089 per cent of the 2013/2014 NHS budget of £112 billion (Lafond, 2015). Pregnant migrants are thus constructed as so threatening that to spend even relatively small proportions of the NHS budget on providing maternity care would be burdensome (Lonergan, 2024b).

The NHS and health citizenship under neoliberalism

Since its creation, then, the NHS has not only been the main institution providing healthcare as a social right of citizenship within the UK; it has been imbricated with racialized and gendered discourses around citizenship and belonging, and in the construction of the boundaries of the 'national home'. As discussed in Chapter 1, discourses and policies around citizenship, including around health citizenship, were reconfigured as a consequence of neoliberal restructuring (Rose, 1999; Bussemaker, 2005). The organization of the NHS and the delivery of healthcare as part of social citizenship was transformed, as was the relationship between the state and citizen regarding the 'vital capacities' of the latter. This had important consequences for the conceptualization and provision of maternity services.

Neoliberal reforms within the NHS

Restructuring within the NHS is an excellent example of what Brenner and Theodore (2002) term 'actually-existing neoliberalism'. Neoliberal restructuring is always implemented within, and shaped and constrained by, an existing political, economic, cultural, and institutional context; the neoliberal 'ideal' can never by fully realized. The centrality of the NHS to British identity has meant that healthcare has remained free at the point of delivery and sheltered the institution from the wholesale privatization to which other some state services were subjected (Cribb, 2008). There is an ongoing debate regarding whether reforms within the NHS can be better described as marketization or privatization, complicated by the fact that the definitions and operationalization of both terms is itself contested (Aldred, 2008; Krachler and Greer, 2015; Waddan, 2018). This book adopts Krachler and Greer's (2015: 216) approach, distinguishing between marketization, which they define as 'a change in transactions, through the introduction or intensification of price-based competition', and privatization, 'a change in ownership in which non-state actors become increasingly involved in provision, usually through a transfer of assets (for example, the sale of a hospital) or an increase in work contracted out'.

Both marketization and privatization have occurred, to a degree, within the NHS. In 1991, the Conservative government introduced an internal market within the NHS, whereby parts of the NHS – initially GPs and District Health Authorities, then Primary Care Trusts, and then Clinical Commissioning Groups – became 'commissioners', purchasing services from other parts of the NHS, namely hospitals and community health services (Pollock et al, 2005; Klein, 2013). Prior to this, District Health Authorities were allocated block funding, which they distributed in their area according to need (Pollock et al, 2005). This internal marketization was strengthened by New Labour (after initial opposition) and a funding structure created whereby the money would 'follow the patient', and there would be payment by results to individual providers (for example, hospitals) (Klein, 2013). This payment structure was supposed to improve services, as it was thought that both commissioners and patients would avoid poorly performing hospitals, which would therefore fail to win contracts and be forced to improve or shut down (Klein, 2013; Allen et al, 2017). The Health and Social Care Act 2012, passed by the Coalition government, further deepened these market reforms. Under the Act, NHS commissioners were required to tender for services, in a process that was subject to EU and UK competition rules, and open to 'any qualified provider' (Allen et al, 2017).[3]

Additionally, the last few decades have seen the increasing involvement of private companies in the provision of both clinical and non-clinical services. According to The King's Fund[4] (2021), in 2019/2020, private providers received 7.2 per cent of NHS commissioners' budget. Arguably, the most visible role of private companies in the NHS has been through Private Finance Initiatives (PFIs). This involves outsourcing 'the design, building, financing and operation' of hospitals and other healthcare services to private companies (The Health Foundation, 2024c; see also Aldred 2008; Klein

2013; Waddan, 2018). This has been done at significant cost; between 2004 and 2021, 99 PFI companies made combined pre-tax profits of almost £2 billion, and paid out dividends of over £1 billion (Centre for Health and Public Interest, 2023).

The provision of healthcare through the NHS was further changed, and healthcare as a right of social citizenship eroded, by the Coalition government's austerity regime. State funding for the NHS had increased significantly under the New Labour government, even as they introduced market reforms; between 1997 and 2010, on average, government funding for the NHS increased 5.5 per cent per year (The King's Fund, 2023). By contrast, between 2010 and 2015, after the introduction of austerity, state funding for the NHS averaged 1.1 per cent per year (The King's Fund, 2023). On the one hand, even this small increase in funding points to the particular status enjoyed by the NHS within the British national imaginary, as most other government departments had suffered swingeing cuts. On the other hand, this increase was still less than the 1.2–1.5 per cent estimated necessary 'just to keep pace with demographic factors' (Baggott, 2016: 102). The NHS was expected to make £20 billion in 'efficiency savings' over 5 years, and as Baggott notes (2016: 113), by 2014/2015, 'the NHS was in serious difficulty, with 40% of NHS trusts and 51% of foundation trusts reporting a deficit for the financial year'. Larger, but still relatively modest, annual increases to the NHS budget were implemented following the election of the Conservative government in 2015, up to 3.4 per cent by 2019 (Gainsbury, 2023). However, by 2014, the NHS began to regularly miss its key performance targets, for example, around waiting times; by the end of 2018/2019, the waiting list for planned care was over 4 million people (including 1,000 who had been waiting for over a year), and as of May 2019, patients were waiting over 4 hours to be seen at most A&E departments (Anandaciva and Ward, 2019; Ham, 2023). In short, it is widely acknowledged that the NHS is in crisis, and has been for several years (Ham, 2023; Anandaciva, 2024), and that health services have become increasingly inaccessible.

Patient choice and the 'responsible' citizen

The crisis within the NHS, and the consequences for healthcare as a right of social citizenship, has arguably been exacerbated by aspects of marketization and privatization within the NHS, which, according to some critics, have diverted resources from patient care to private companies (particularly with regard to PFIs) and to the bureaucracy required to manage the 'internal market' (Pollock et al, 2005; Centre for Health and Public Interest, 2023; Rowland, 2023). Furthermore, market reforms within the NHS have been accompanied by a wider shift in the construction of 'health citizenship', and the understanding of the role of the state and the individual regarding the health and 'vital capacities' of the latter. As discussed in Chapter 1, the implementation of neoliberal economic restructuring in the UK and other wealthy countries was accompanied by a shift in discourses around citizenship, which stressed the 'responsibilities' of citizenship over the entitlements, and in which the 'ideal citizen' was constructed as self-managing, entrepreneurial, and economically productive (Rose, 1999; Nyers, 2004; van Houdt et al, 2011). The responsibilities of this 'ideal citizen' extended to the management of their health. Crawford (1980) argues that, in many wealthy countries, the 1960s and 1970s saw both the emergence of a greater consciousness with regard to personal health and, by the late 1970s, the construction of health as a personal moral responsibility and duty – what he refers to as 'healthism' (Crawford, 2006; Brown and Baker, 2012; Cairns and Johnston, 2015). In the UK (not just England), this was also the period in which two separate, but related, patients' rights movements emerged. The first focused on the patient as an autonomous individual, with the right to determine what happened to their body, including with regard to medical care. This was the ethos of the Patients Association, founded in 1963 following the revelation that 'NHS patients were routinely being used in medical experiments without their knowledge or consent (Pappworth, 1962)' (Mold, 2010: 510). The second movement focused on the rights of patients as taxpayers, who had the right to have an input into how health services were provided, given that their taxes were paying for said services (Mold, 2010). This consumerist idea of patients' rights was co-opted by the Thatcher government in justifying their early neoliberal reforms to the NHS (Mold, 2010).

In neoliberal discourses around health citizenship, individuals are constructed as rational 'citizen-consumers', who seek out the information necessary to make 'good choices' regarding their health; the role of the state is to provide these 'citizen-consumers' with appropriate information in making 'good choices' and otherwise deploy a range of technologies in order to influence individuals' decision-making (Brown and Baker, 2012; Crawshaw, 2013; Cairns and Johnston, 2015; Brookes, 2021). Brown and Baker (2012: 23), for example, quote the 2009 NHS constitution, in encouraging citizens to take responsibility for their health: 'You should recognise that you can make a significant contribution to your own, and your family's, good health and well-being, and take some personal responsibility for it.' (Department of Health, 2009: 9)

For some patients, the greater range of choices, and even the encouragement to have more responsibility and involvement in one's health and medical treatment, can be experienced as empowering (Rier, 2022). However, wider social determinants of poor health are largely ignored, as are the obstacles to accessing health services created by funding cuts (Crawshaw, 2013; Brookes, 2021). This is particularly significant at present, given the impact on public health of over a decade of austerity (Schrecker and Bambra, 2015; Marmot et al, 2020). Individuals who fail to conform to discourses of responsible health citizenship, whether by choice or due to structural obstacles, may be seen as at fault for their poor health, subject to disciplinary pressure to make 'better choices', and, in extreme cases, denied access to care (Brown and Baker, 2012; Brookes, 2021).

Moreover, within England, the responsibility of the 'good' healthy citizen may also extend to improving and protecting the NHS. As discussed above, a system of 'payment by results' was implemented as part of the marketization of the NHS. Patients, therefore, are expected to make rational, informed choices regarding care, not only as part of their responsibility for their own health, but also to ensure that 'good' secondary care providers are financially rewarded, and poor providers penalized. This expectation may be reinforced by the peculiar place of the NHS in national imaginary, with citizens called upon to make 'good choices' to safeguard 'our (underfunded) NHS', thereby absolving the state of responsibility for maintaining health services (Brookes, 2021; Spratt, 2022). The extent to which 'patient choice' functions as a quality control mechanism is questionable. As Pollock et al (2005) point out, geographically speaking some hospitals cannot be closed because there are no other options within reasonable travel distance. Furthermore, patients may not have the clinical knowledge to make informed choices about secondary care providers; citing Dixon et al (2010), Davies (2013: 571–572) states: 'In practice, it seems probable that most patients will prefer to be guided by their GP or to make choices on practical grounds, such as ease of travelling to the hospital.'

NHS maternity services and responsible reproductive citizenship

Neoliberal discourses around choice and 'responsibility' have also become embedded within NHS maternity policies and practices. As part of their responsibility for reproducing the nation state, pregnant women have long been constructed as accountable for the health of the foetus and newborn baby; the 'bad mothering' practices of working class women were blamed for high infant mortality rates in the Edwardian era, for example (Davin, 1978; McIntosh, 2012). However, as discussed in Chapter 1, at present, 'responsible reproductive citizenship' involves parenting in accordance with wider neoliberal norms of citizenship, for example, by being in paid work and minimizing the level of support one receives from the state. In keeping with the evolution of 'health citizenship' under neoliberalism, women and other birthing people are therefore expected to take responsibility for ensuring they receive the best possible maternity care. While in the past, responsible reproductive citizenship may have required a pregnant woman to submit to a doctor's judgement, under neoliberalism, pregnant women are expected to be informed, engaged 'choosers', deploying their power as consumers to safeguard both their health and that of their foetus, and to improve NHS maternity services (Browne, 2016). Examining policy and practice around maternity care in England, it is thus possible to identify the emergence of an 'ideal birthing citizen', the 'default' consumer of maternity services, and the model of the person who 'should' be reproducing the nation state. This 'ideal birthing citizen', who is the main focus of Chapter 5, is a woman who reproduces responsibly, engages with NHS maternity services, and makes 'good choices' for both herself and her baby. She is also, as I note later, a white British citizen.

Maternity care in England at present is usually led by midwives, unless the birthing person is deemed to have a 'high risk' pregnancy, in which case their care may be supervised by an obstetrician. Birthing people are expected to register with a midwife by the time they are 12 weeks pregnant. In a 'low-risk' pregnancy, the birthing person will begin by seeing their midwife monthly, then more frequently in the third trimester, and will usually have two ultrasound scans, one at 12 weeks and one at 20 weeks (NHS, n.d.). An individual with a low-risk pregnancy usually has the choice of giving birth in a maternity ward, at home, or in a birthing centre – a unit run by midwives where limited medical intervention can take place (NHS, 2024). The birthing centre or maternity ward need not be the one closest to the birthing person's house, but can be outside of their local trust. Ideally, there should be 'continuity of carer', whereby one midwife is responsible for a pregnant woman through her antenatal and perinatal care, although it is acknowledged that this is not yet occurring in many areas (National Maternity Review, 2016).

The paradigm for the delivery of maternity care in England is that of 'personalized care' as outlined in *Better Births*, the 2016 National Maternity Review for England (National Maternity Review, 2016: 8). Personalized maternity care is 'centred on the woman, her baby and her family, based around their needs and their decisions, where they have genuine choice, informed by unbiased information' (8). The 'unbiased information' is to be made available by midwives and other clinical staff, as well as through 'access to a comprehensive digital tool that offers them the information they need throughout pregnancy' (52). Indeed, pregnant women are constructed as '"savvy consumers" of online information' (34; see also Browne, 2016). Pregnant women are encouraged to use this information to make decisions about their pregnancy and care, including where they will receive care and give birth (National Maternity Review, 2016: 43).

However, in keeping with neoliberal discourses and practices around health citizenship, the right to make choices about one's care is accompanied by the expectation that one makes 'good choices' in order to secure maternal health. In fact, 'choice' is presented as not only critical to the health of the individual woman, but to the delivery of NHS maternity services in general. Pregnant women (and their families) are called to be 'powerful agents for change ... by making well-informed choices to ensure safe, personalized care is built around them' (National Maternity Review, 2016: 84). Furthermore, because the 'money follows the patient', this is supposed to ensure that 'better' maternity hospitals are financially rewarded, while poorer hospitals will be forced to improve their services.

Wider social determinants of maternal health, and obstacles to engaging with NHS maternity services, tend to be overlooked within *Better Births*, beyond those that are most easily reduced to 'individual choice', like quitting smoking. It is acknowledged within the review that 'vulnerable women may need extra support to [engage with maternity services]' (National Maternity Review, 2016: 84), but the extra support suggested appears to largely consist of health professionals keeping an open mind and spending more time speaking with the woman in question, although specialist services are recommended for the particularly vulnerable. Similarly, it is claimed that breastfeeding provides 'a natural safety net against the worst effects of poverty' (National Maternity Review, 2016: 63–64); the role of the individual in making 'good choices' in order to overcome poverty is centred, rather than a discussion of the impact of government policies, such as austerity.

Strikingly, while pregnant migrants featured prominently in wider debates around NHS bordering and the association between the NHS and the 'national home', they are virtually absent from *Better Births*. The specific challenges facing pregnant migrants are not discussed, beyond an assertion that 'families from Black and Minority Ethnic (BME) backgrounds' might, in some cases, require healthcare providers to '[take] the extra time to gauge understanding of the language being used at an appointment' (36). This clearly conflates 'migrant' and 'BME', in keeping with wider racialized discourses of citizenship and belonging. Additionally, there is no discussion of racism, and indeed only a brief consideration of the specific needs of racially minoritized women, and the largest part of this occurs in a section titled 'Care for women with different backgrounds' (35), thereby implying that the 'standard' woman is white.

Conclusion

Health and healthcare are inextricably entangled with gendered, racialized, and classed discourses of citizenship, and the construction of the boundaries of national belonging. Indeed, the NHS, since its inception, has been implicated in contestations around national identity and the 'national home'. Given the intertwined and mutually constitutive relationship between discourses and policies around reproduction, and those around citizenship, it is not surprising that anxieties around the reproduction have figured prominently in these contestations, and in the use of the NHS to demarcate the boundaries of national belonging. Pregnant migrants as a threat to both the NHS and the wider national home figured prominently in Parliamentary debates and policy documents around the introduction of stricter NHS bordering in the Immigration Act 2014.

Even as the provision of healthcare has been deployed in defining the boundaries of national belonging, the way this healthcare is delivered, and the relationship between healthcare and citizenship, has been transformed by neoliberal restructuring. Discourses of 'healthism' (Crawford, 1980) construct health as the moral obligation of individual citizens, erasing the impact of wider social determinants of health. Moreover, in England, following the introduction of an 'internal market' within the NHS, 'patient choice' is treated as a quality control mechanism. Consequently, English health citizenship at present involves not only making 'good choices' to safeguard one's health, but to improve NHS services. This neoliberal model of health citizenship has had an important influence on the conceptualization of maternity service provision, with pregnant women called upon to be 'agents for change' by making good choices, even as structural obstacles to accessing maternity services are largely ignored and the 'standard' pregnant woman is assumed to be a white citizen.

The following three chapters of this book explore how policies and discourses around citizenship and belonging interact with racialized, neoliberal models of health citizenship in shaping migrants' experiences of pregnancy and maternity care. I begin by looking at how bordering processes are underpinned by a heteronormative, white nuclear family model, and how these processes differentially distribute resources required for reproductive autonomy and discipline migrant women's reproductive practices and family building projects. Chapters 4 and 5 then look more specifically at access to, and experiences of, antenatal and maternity care. Chapter 4 argues that bordering processes serve as instruments of stratified reproduction, limiting some pregnant migrants' access to NHS maternity services, and that this is exacerbated by the 'personalized care' paradigm, which calls upon pregnant women to be 'informed, engaged choosers' while disregarding this stratification. Chapter 5 builds upon this, looking at the provision of maternity services through the lens of citizenship, and arguing that pregnant migrants who are unwilling or unable to behave as the 'ideal birthing citizen' may receive substandard care and/or find their reproductive autonomy disregarded.

3

Family Bordering, Reproductive Autonomy, and Migrant Women's Experiences of Pregnancy and New Motherhood

Introduction

This chapter explores the impact of family bordering processes on my participants' reproductive autonomy and experiences of pregnancy and maternity care. Family bordering processes reflect and reinforce the association between liberal citizenship and the white, patriarchal, heteronormative nuclear family (Turner, 2015; 2017; 2020). Through these processes, some families and family forms are constructed as compatible with citizenship and the 'correct' reproduction of the nation state, and others as illegitimate or even threatening to the national reproductive future. Family bordering created significant reproductive injustice and stratification for my participants, shaping their decisions around reproduction and their access to support through wider family networks. Despite the exclusion many of my participants faced, however, they continued to assert their presence as individuals reproducing the next generation of British citizens, negotiating the constraints placed upon their reproductive decision-making and developing networks of support within the UK.

In this chapter, I take a broad definition of family bordering processes as encompassing any processes, practices, and policies that dictate the terms on which migrants can live with their families in the UK. As I outline in more detail later, this definition includes family visas, as well as other visas, such as work visas, that may allow the holder to be accompanied by dependents. UK citizens are also impacted by family bordering processes, for example, if they wish to marry a non-citizen.

Within discourses and policies around citizenship and bordering, migrants may be constructed as more or less desirable based on whether they are perceived as doing family 'correctly'; at the same time, having one's family ties recognized and respected is a marker of citizenship and belonging, for both legal citizens and migrants (Erel, 2018; Turner, 2020). Because the nuclear family is constructed as the 'legitimate' site for the reproduction of the nation state, family bordering processes are informed by anxieties around reproduction and the capacities of some migrants to reproduce the nation state 'correctly.' Concurrently, in determining who can live in a particular country with their families, and on what terms, family bordering processes discipline migrant family forms and reproductive practices. These processes differentially distribute state support for reproduction, for example, in the UK, through No Recourse to Public Funds policies. They also influence the availability and nature of family support for reproduction, by setting conditions on which family members are allowed to live together, or even visit, conditions which reflect wider racialized, gendered, and neoliberal discourses around what constitutes a legitimate family. This is especially relevant during pregnancy, childbirth, and new parenthood as major life events that may involve extended family networks. Indeed, *Better Births*, the 2016 National Maternity Review for England, assumes that pregnant and birthing women are supported by family and make decisions based on what is best for their entire family. The contrast between these assumptions and the lived reality of many of my participants highlights the extent to which migrants are excluded from the construction of the 'ideal birthing citizen'.

I begin this chapter by outlining the emergence, under liberalism, of the heteronormative nuclear family as the 'legitimate' site for the reproduction of the nation state; its gendered, classed, and racialized underpinnings; and its evolution into the 'procreative couple form' (Roseneil et al, 2020). I then discuss how family bordering processes in the UK, historically and at present, have been informed by anxieties around the reproduction of the nation state, before moving on to explore my participants' experiences of reproductive injustice and reproductive stratification as a consequence of these processes. Family bordering processes emerged as a key factor in the reproductive decision-making of some of my participants. The conditions attached to heteronormative nuclear family life in the UK by bordering processes can keep spouses apart, denying women and other birthing people the support of their husbands or partners in pregnancy and childbirth. Finally, family bordering processes in the UK do not recognize family ties outside of the nuclear family; most visas do not permit the sponsorship of extended family members, and these members are only allowed to visit so long as they are not perceived as potential overstayers. This ensures that some migrants are denied the in-person support of their extended family during pregnancy, childbirth, and new motherhood. However, the women I interviewed did their best to maintain contact with family transnationally through communications technology, and to forge new networks of support within the UK.

Citizenship, reproduction, and the family

In the UK and many other countries, citizenship has become intertwined with a heteronormative nuclear family form that is heavily racialized, gendered, and classed, and produces individuals into different roles with regard to the reproduction of the nation state. The advent of liberal citizenship was accompanied by the emergence of the heteronormative nuclear family as 'the "natural" unit of human intimacy' (Turner, 2020: 42; see also Peterson, 2020). This construction of the heteronormative nuclear family as the 'correct' family form enabled the state 'to codify a distinction between "legitimate" and "other" (non-conforming, inferior) sexual/ conjugal practices, thus establishing state-sanctioned lines of descent' (Peterson, 2020: 190–191).

The heteronormative nuclear family, therefore, became the legitimate site for the reproduction of the nation state, both biologically and socially, and played a key role in the construction of hierarchical and multi-tiered discourses around citizenship and reproduction. The nuclear family was central to the maintenance of the public/private gendered dichotomy constitutive of liberalism, discussed in Chapter 1, and the construction of women as responsible for biological and social reproduction. The codification of the nuclear family as the 'legitimate' family form also made it a key vehicle for the generational transmission of wealth, thereby facilitating the regulation of inheritance of property and wealth necessary for maintaining capitalism (Collins, 1998; Peterson, 2020; Turner, 2020). As part of this, the nuclear family became classed, associated with bourgeois respectability (Roseneil et al, 2020); the construction of the working classes as undomesticated and unruly contributed to anxieties that they could not reproduce the nation state 'correctly' (Davin, 1978; McClintock, 1995; Turner, 2017).

Furthermore, the construction of the heteronormative nuclear family as the 'ideal' family form played a critical role in the development of 'race' and racism, and was central to racialized discourses and practices of British and European colonialism (Peterson, 2020; Turner, 2020). The family forms and practices of colonized people were contrasted with, and deemed inferior to, the white, Christian heteronormative nuclear family, and this, in turn, was used as 'proof' of the general superiority of Europeans. Similarly, the notion of 'romantic love' between spouses as the basis for a marriage came to be associated with whiteness and constructed as 'superior' to other reasons for marriage, including property relations or sexual attraction (d'Aoust, 2018; Pellander, 2021). At the same time, regulations around marriage and intimacy in colonies strengthened the racialization of the nuclear family as 'white', and deployed the family in maintaining divisions between colonizer and colonized (Turner, 2015; 2020). Finally, colonized and enslaved persons were constructed as abject and 'other' by destroying their existing familial and kin relations, and denying their ability to form such relations, including parental relations (Turner, 2020). The trans-Atlantic slave trade involved the destruction of African families and the refusal to recognize or respect whatever kinship and intimate relationships enslaved peoples formed (Roberts, 2017; Turner, 2020; Spillers, 2022).

Although the heteronormative nuclear family model has evolved in many countries over the last several decades, its fundamental scaffolding, including its gendered, racialized, and classed underpinnings, has persisted. This includes its role as the appropriate site for the biological and social reproduction of the nation state. Indeed, discussing the 'tenacity of the couple-norm' in Europe, Roseneil et al (2020: 21) write: 'cohabiting, *procreative* coupledom remains the privileged and normative form of intimate life: the good and proper intimate citizen is no longer necessarily married or heterosexual, but they are living in a long-term, stable, sexually exclusive, co-residential partnership' (emphasis added).

With regard to the UK, as discussed in Chapter 1, the post-war welfare state was constructed around, and supported, a heteronormative nuclear family with a male breadwinner and a dependent female homemaker, and in doing so, structured particular dynamics and practices around reproduction (Pateman, 1989; Lister, 2003; Bhattacharyya, 2015; Roseneil et al, 2020). This has evolved, under neoliberal restructuring, to a family model where it is presumed, and expected, that both adults are in paid labour (Lonergan, 2015; Roseneil et al, 2020). Nonetheless, women continue to be constructed as responsible for biological and social reproduction, a responsibility that has taken on new significance with welfare state retrenchment (Feminist Fightback, 2011; Bhattacharyya, 2015; Bassel and Emejulu, 2017). Similarly, the 'procreative couple form' continues to be associated with middle-class 'respectability' and is used to discipline and stigmatize the reproductive practices of single working-class mothers, as when then Prime Minister David Cameron suggested families without fathers were to blame for the 2011 riots (Jensen, 2012; Roseneil et al, 2020). While mixed marriages are now common in the UK, and the heteronormative nuclear family less explicitly racialized, as I outline below, the model continues to play an important role in bordering processes that associate Britishness with whiteness, and construct racially minoritized migrants as threatening social cohesion and national reproductive futures (Wray, 2011; Byrne, 2015; Turner, 2015; 2020). Even the expansion of the nuclear family to include same-sex couples served to reaffirm the cohabiting, monogamous couple as the ideal family form; David Cameron framed his support for the legalization of same-sex marriage as reflecting his support for legal monogamous marriage more broadly (Roseneil et al, 2020).

Family bordering and reproduction in the UK

Family bordering is one of the principle ways in which the state seeks to regulate the family and its role in the reproduction of the nation state. Family migration poses a particular challenge to the maintenance of the boundaries of the nation state, and the national reproductive future, because claims to entry and settlement are initially, at least, based on choices individuals have made about their families and relationships rather than state criteria (Wray, 2011). Before proceeding, it is useful to outline how family bordering processes are conceptualized within this chapter. I take a broad view of family bordering as encompassing all processes and policies that determine whether, and on what terms, people who consider themselves to be family can live together and/or visit each other in a country, in this case, the UK. The family ties under discussion, therefore, are not limited to those of the heteronormative nuclear family. Family bordering includes:

- Spousal and family visas, where an individual with UK citizenship or Indefinite Leave to Remain (ILR) wishes to live, in the UK, with a person they consider family, whether a spouse, child, or other relative;
- Policies determining which migrants are able to bring 'dependents' and who qualifies as a dependent, for example, with regard to work visas;
- Policies facilitating, or not, family reunification of individuals living in the UK, especially refugees, with family members abroad;
- And policies facilitating, or not, visits between individuals living in the UK and family members living abroad.

This last point may seem outside the remit of family migration as the family members in question are not seeking to live in the UK; however, as I demonstrate later, these policies shape the construction and maintenance of family ties, and the family support available to individuals in the UK, including pregnant migrants.

Family bordering in the UK is underpinned by the white heteronormative nuclear model, and its more recent version, the 'procreative couple form' (Roseneil et al, 2020). Historically, and at present, migrants have been judged as suitable for entry and settlement, or not, based on whether their family forms conform to this model (Samantrai, 2002; Turner, 2020). Family visas, for example, can be used to sponsor spouses and dependent children, but not usually extended family members[1] (Gov. uk, n.d.-b). At the same time, the recognition of one's family ties is a marker of citizenship, and the conditional and selective (non)recognition of these ties central to the creation of different immigration categories, the disciplining of migrants, and the construction of the continuum of exclusion/inclusion around citizenship. Individuals on highly skilled workers' visas are allowed to bring dependent spouses and children (for a steep cost), for example, but individuals on short-term seasonal worker visas are not. This serves to distinguish between the former group as 'desirable' migrants and potential future citizens, and the latter group as a disposable reserve army of temporary labour. Family bordering processes are informed by anxieties around migrants' reproductive practices, because of the importance of the family in organizing the reproduction of the nation state (Gedalof, 2007; Lonergan, 2018), and also shape migrants' reproductive practices and experiences of reproduction, by determining which families are able to live in the UK and on what terms, and the level of state support to which they are entitled (Colen, 1995; Bonizzoni, 2011). Critically, it is not only migrants but citizens who are affected by family migration policies. Family bordering processes thus contribute to the construction of citizenship as hierarchical and multi-tiered by differentiating between those citizens who are able to build a family life in the UK and those who are not.

Gender, race, neoliberalism, and evolving paradigms of family bordering

UK immigration policies in the 1960s and 1970s were informed by a construction of the 'ideal' British family as white, patriarchal, and nuclear. Family migration from 'new' Commonwealth countries was viewed with considerable ambivalence by the state: on the one hand, the 'migrant wife' and 'migrant family' were seen as blunting the 'threat' posed to white British women by the black or Asian male migrant worker, and preventing miscegenation; on the other hand, the migrant family was also seen as 'unfamilial' and strange, and potentially undermining the white heteronormative British nuclear family, and by extension, white British society (Wray, 2011; Turner, 2015; 2020). Anxiety about the reproductive practices of migrant families also played a role in these policies. The claim that the Caribbean had high rates of illegitimate birth was used in debates around the Commonwealth Immigrants Act 1962 to construct Caribbean migrants as unsuitable for life in the UK (Samantrai, 2002). In keeping with the patriarchal nature of the nuclear family, it was assumed in this era that 'legitimate' migration for the purposes of family reunification was undertaken by women, and permitting men to settle in the UK to join their wives was treated as a 'special concession' rather than part of the right to family life (Samantrai, 2002; Wray, 2011). From 1969 to 1974, male Commonwealth citizens were in fact barred from joining their wives in the UK, with an exception made for those 'presenting special features' (Wray, 2011: 48; see also Samantrai, 2002).

As discussed in Chapter 1, New Labour's 'managed migration' scheme marked a significant departure from previous immigration regimes, as it was premised on the idea that migration by highly skilled, economically productive individuals could be beneficial to the UK. This new approach significantly reconfigured family bordering processes, and the disciplining of migrants' reproductive activities through these processes. The right to a family life for migrants and citizens with migrant family members became dependent upon demonstrating that one's family would be economically productive (Sirriyeh, 2015). This included the expectation that families with migrant members would reproduce 'responsibly', without burdening the welfare state (Lonergan, 2018). Individuals who met the criteria to be considered 'highly skilled workers' were able to be accompanied by their spouse and dependent children but not other family members, reflecting the construction of the nuclear family as the 'proper' family form. However, they and their dependents were not able to claim public funds, nor were individuals on family visas. The requirement that the migrant family be economically self-sufficient was further entrenched under the Coalition and, later, Conservative governments. From 2012, citizens or settled residents wishing to sponsor a spouse were required to demonstrate a minimum income of £18,600,[2] as this was the level at which most couples would no longer qualify for income-related benefits (Home Office, 2012). Similarly, visa fees rose exponentially under the Coalition and Conservative governments, and the introduction of the Immigration Health Surcharge further increased the cost of sponsoring a spouse, or migrating with one's spouse and children. The high cost of work and family visas effectively required families with migrant members to be able to reproduce 'responsibly', ensuring that the cost of an additional dependent, or income lost to maternity leave, would not put them at risk of losing their visa status (Lonergan, 2018). Recently, the Conservative government has announced plans to raise the minimum income required to sponsor a spouse to £29,000, with plans to eventually raise it to £38,700. Strikingly, £38,700 is also the recently announced minimum threshold to qualify for a skilled worker visa; British citizens must therefore be considered 'skilled workers' (or at least earn the same amount) to exercise their right to a family life (Jorgensen, 2024).

The managed migration paradigm also marked a break from previous immigration policy regimes in that it was, ostensibly, racially neutral – the 'highly skilled migrant' might be of any ethnicity or nationality. However, as discussed in Chapter 1, racially minoritized migrants, especially Muslim migrants, were constructed as introducing an untenable level of 'difference' in the UK, disrupting social cohesion and, in the case of Muslims, posing a potential terrorist threat (Burnett, 2004; Worley, 2005; Fortier, 2010). Family bordering processes reflected anxieties about the 'unfamilial' racially minoritized migrant family and their reproductive practices. Migration for arranged marriages was subject to particular scrutiny under New Labour and subsequent governments as both indicative of a failure by British Asians to properly 'integrate', and inherently suspicious and potentially fraudulent (Gedalof, 2007; Wray, 2011; Byrne, 2015). Racially minoritized migrant wives were similarly constructed as threatening social cohesion by failing to reproduce 'correctly' and thereby preventing their (British-born) children from 'integrating' (Yuval-Davis et al, 2005; Gedalof, 2007). The latter anxieties were especially expressed through concerns about the English language capabilities of female family migrants. Official discussions around the New Labour immigration white paper Secure Borders, Safe Haven: Integration with Diversity in Modern Britain (Home Office, 2002) suggested that the 2001 urban disturbances may have been partly caused by the lack of English language skills among the British Asian rioters' mothers and grandmothers (Yuval-Davis et al, 2005; Bassel and Khan, 2021). New Labour introduced a requirement that any individual on a family migration visa applying for ILR demonstrate English language skills at a basic level; this was later increased to an intermediate level by the Coalition government (Sirriyeh, 2015).[3]

The proliferation of bordering processes in recent years has multiplied the conditions to which migrant families may be subject, and intensified the surveillance and disciplining of migrant families and their reproductive practices. Prior to 2003, an individual on a spousal visa, for example, qualified for ILR after 1 year of residency in the UK; from 2003 to 2012, this period of residency was extended to 2 years, with applicants required to pass a language test and/ or the Life in the UK Test since 2007 (Sirriyeh, 2015). Since 2012, a person on a spousal visa must wait 5 years before qualifying for ILR; reapply for their visa after 30 months, meeting the minimum household income requirement discussed above and paying all related visa fees, including the Immigration Health Surcharge; and pass the Life in the UK Test *and* demonstrate English fluency at intermediate level. During this 5-year period, the migrant spouse has No Recourse to Public Funds. As I discuss in more detail later, this intensification of bordering processes can have a significant impact on decisions around family planning and reproductive autonomy (see also Lonergan, 2018).

In the rest of this chapter, I explore the impact of family bordering processes on my participants' experiences of family planning, pregnancy, and childbirth. These processes interacted with multiple other factors, including my participants' visa status, country of origin, and proximity to family and friends, as well as the availability of local support, in producing both reproductive injustice in the form of significant constraints on reproductive and bodily autonomy, and reproductive stratification.

'Carrying' the weight of family planning under the spectre of the border

Sarah Marie Hall (2023) has developed the concept of 'carrying' to denote the combination of emotional, embodied, and relational labour involved in social reproduction and reproductive decision-making under austerity. Hall's (2023: 42) research participants discussed the physical and emotional toll involved in planning for potential reproductive futures while coping with the instabilities produced by neoliberal restructuring: 'The various carryings associated with reproduction and reproductive decisions can be a bodily toll, an embodied and visceral strain, and with gendered, racialised, classed, intergenerational and emplaced implications.'

The concept of 'carrying' provides a good framework for considering the effect of bordering processes on some of my participants' reproductive decision-making and reproductive autonomy. 'Carrying' brings together an analysis of the role of structural factors in constraining and shaping reproductive decision-making and autonomy – congruent with the overall reproductive justice lens deployed in this book – with a focus on the embodied physical and psychological toll of these constraints, and how this is experienced differently by individuals depending upon their social location. Moreover, 'carrying' is specifically interested in the embodied and visceral labour around reproductive futures, and the logistical and emotional challenges of trying to make reproductive plans in a highly uncertain environment. For some women I interviewed, the cost of visa renewals and the necessity of maintaining a minimum household income (for those on spousal visas) were key factors to be considered when planning pregnancies. In this way, they were disciplined by bordering processes into demonstrating they could reproduce 'responsibly', in keeping with neoliberal discourses of citizenship. More than this, however, bordering processes were described as something that had to be carried constantly in the back of one's mind when thinking about the future, including reproductive futures; the years of precarity, the necessity to reapply at regular intervals, and the associated bureaucratic hurdles all contributed to creating these processes as an ongoing source of stress.

The emotional weight of bordering processes, and its role in constraining reproductive decision-making, is illuminated by Ayetree's experience. Ayetree had come to the UK on a student visa, but was on a spousal visa at the time of her pregnancy. In her interview, she emphasized bordering processes as something that had to be planned for constantly, including with regard to pregnancy. She stated: 'Anybody I speak to who is an immigrant has to have at the back of their head a plan for money.' She explained how that had affected her family planning decisions:

> You do not have a choice. You have to plan around it. Because having a baby itself was planning in terms of when we got the spouse visa versus what our age was, what our monetary status, where my job was, where his job was. It was like a plan, if it didn't latch in the first two months, we would have carried on trying. But it's something you are constantly thinking, now I'm going for an ILR, so it's like, you save for the first spouse visa then from the point you get the first spouse visa, you save for the second spouse visa. From the point you get the second spouse visa, you save for the ILR. From the point you get the ILR, you save for if you want to save for a citizenship.

She later elaborated:

> But because our case was straightforward, we thought, okay, at this point, if we do manage to get pregnancy, so in our second, by the time we get our spouse second renewal, we should have our new baby. But, having said that, I will also tell you at the back of my mind, because you are an immigrant and you constantly think about these things, I was like, is this the right decision? Having pregnancy even before second renewal? What if we don't get the second renewal and I have to go back to [country of origin]?

Bordering processes may additionally interact with other structural factors in creating reproductive injustice and reproductive stratification. Immigration policies, for example, can render people dependent upon their employers, restricting their reproductive autonomy. Emily is a white North American in the UK on a work visa, and married to a UK citizen. The conditions of her Tier 2 work visa, in combination with the prevalence of contract work in her sector, shaped her experiences of pregnancy and created an ever-present source of concern. She explained:

> [C]ertainly planning maternity leave has been a big part of – Like because my ability to stay in the UK is tied to my employment, I think one of the things I was really worried about initially was that I knew that my contract was coming to an end when I would want to be on maternity leave so one of the things I talked to my HR department about was you know, can they kick me out while I'm on – You know because I wouldn't necessarily be able to go sort a new [employment] contract.

She echoed Ayetree's sense of bordering processes as an enduring source of stress, always at the back of one's mind:

But I think that was like a source of uncertainty for a little while, which meant like pregnancy and sort of like an intersection of like thinking about maternity leave and pregnancy with the sort of hanging, you know, sort of ever present concern about like; am I complying with immigration rules?

Bordering processes, 'the family', and reproductive citizenship

Bordering processes may also limit the family support available to migrants during pregnancy, childbirth, and new motherhood. As noted earlier, the heteronormative nuclear family is constructed as the legitimate site for the reproduction of the nation state, and privileged above other family forms in bordering processes. For families with migrant members, the right to a life with one's spouse and children is nonetheless highly conditional, and these conditions are informed by, among other factors, racialized and classed anxieties around the reproductive practices of these families (Erel, 2018). In some circumstances, this may lead to a pregnant person being separated from their spouse. At the same time, the privileging of the nuclear family can serve to additionally stratify reproduction by limiting support available from extended family networks. With the reconfiguration of the nuclear family norm to one with two breadwinners in much of the Global North, and wide national and local variations in the availability of state-subsided childcare (Gromada and Richardson, 2021), extended family members take an active role in raising children. Childcare is often very expensive in the UK (Reis and Stephens, 2022), and unsurprisingly, the 2022 Childcare and Early Years Survey of Parents conducted by the Department of Education (2023) revealed that 17 per cent of children receive informal childcare from grandparents. As well, women's mothers, in particular, may play an important role in providing practical and emotional support during pregnancy and new motherhood (Deave et al, 2008). Yet, for families with migrant members, the possibility of even being visited by one's extended family during the transition to motherhood is highly stratified according to class, immigration status, and country of origin.

Separation from one's spouse

Family bordering processes, in extreme circumstances, can lead to a woman being separated from her husband during pregnancy, during childbirth, and in new motherhood, stratifying the support available to her during these times. It is important not to romanticize the role of spouses and the nuclear family in providing support for pregnant women. There is an extensive literature discussing the ways in which family migration policies reinforce the patriarchal foundations of the nuclear family, disadvantaging women and rendering them more vulnerable to domestic violence (see Burman and Chantler, 2005; Anitha, 2008; Dudley, 2017). However, migrant and racially minoritized women have also sought to problematize and nuance mainstream feminist arguments around the heteronormative nuclear family as a source of patriarchal oppression by pointing out the devaluing of racialized and migrant nuclear families in a range of government policies (see Amos and Parmar, 1984; Bhavnani and Coulson, 1986). Moreover, many of the women I interviewed *did* specifically cite their husbands as an important source of emotional and practical support during pregnancy.

The experience of reproductive stratification produced by being separated from one's partner by bordering processes will be further variegated by the visa status and social location of different women and the resources available to them. Two of the women I interviewed, Amina and Maram, found themselves separated from their partner in the latter stages of pregnancy and while giving birth, because of bordering processes. However, Amina was from a relatively privileged background in her country of origin and had the support of extended family in the UK, while Maram was in an extremely precarious position in both her country of origin and in the UK, which exacerbated the effect of being separated from her husband.

Amina is originally from a Middle Eastern country, and had lived and worked in a well-paying profession for several years in another Middle Eastern country before moving to the UK. She and her husband, who is from the same country, have three children, the youngest of whom was born in the UK. Amina's husband successfully applied for a Tier 1 (investor) visa,[4] with Amina and their two older children included on the visa as his dependents. Amina and her two children arrived in the UK several months before her husband, while Amina was heavily pregnant. She gave birth less than a month after arriving. The decision to go ahead of her husband and give birth in the UK was made in part because of concerns about whether their visa would allow them to enter the country with a third child. During our interview, when I noted that she had given birth soon after entering the UK, Amina explained:

Amina:	Yeah… before my delivery, and because new baby, it's hard to deliver outside the UK, then how about the paper and the BRP [Biometric Residence Permit], you know? That's why I'm worried. That's why I make carrier before I get to delivery.
Gwyneth:	So you made sure you arrived before you were going to have the baby?
Amina:	Yeah, that's why.

As with the work visa, the investor visa required high fees for each dependent, as part of disciplining migrants into demonstrating economic productivity; bringing a new baby would have been expensive, or even required a new application.

While Amina, like many other women discussed in this chapter, had to ensure her family met the criteria of relevant visa schemes when making plans around reproduction, Maram was in a far more precarious situation, excluded from visa schemes designed to provide migrants with a route to settle in the UK with their families. Maram is an asylum seeker, originally from a Middle Eastern country where she is part of a severely marginalized ethnic group and is de facto stateless even within her country of origin. This emerged during the interview when she was discussing her experiences of home births in her country of origin and revealed she did not have the papers that would allow her to go to hospital. Maram's effective statelessness meant neither she nor her husband would be able to demonstrate the economic productivity required to qualify for any visa schemes. Additionally, because she is unable to access travel documents, expanding bordering processes left her no choice but to travel overland across Europe to the UK. Even if her family could afford plane tickets, the Immigration (Carriers Liability) Act 1987 allows the UK government to fine airlines who bring people without visas to the UK, incentivizing airlines to prevent people without visas from boarding. Maram and her four children became separated from her husband at some point during their journey; she realized she was pregnant a few weeks after arriving in the UK and applying for asylum.

While both women had to deal with being separated from their husbands, and made it clear that they found this distressing, Amina had access to far more resources and support than Maram. Amina and her children stayed with her husband's cousin and his family. Her cousin-in-law explained how to register with his GP, critically important for a heavily pregnant woman; her cousin-in-law's wife also accompanied her through childbirth; and the family watched her children while she was in hospital. Nonetheless, Amina discussed feeling overwhelmed by the treatment choices she was offered during labour, and that this was exacerbated by her husband's absence. Furthermore, Amina needed stitches after giving birth, and despite feeling that something was wrong with the stitches, she decided not to say anything to hospital staff because she was concerned for her two other children and wanted to return to her cousin-in-law's house as soon as possible:

Gwyneth: So you felt – you felt that there was something wrong with the suture she did?

Amina: Yeah.

Gwyneth: And did you tell people at the hospital about that?

Amina:　　　　　No, I didn't tell them, because actually I... at this moment, I want to finish, because I want to come back to the home, my kids. I leave them with my cousins, and they used to, they used – I have to sleep with them... I am – I'm thinking about a whole lot of things.

Maram, by contrast, was very isolated and relied heavily on local community organizations, her midwife, and a social worker, to attend her antenatal appointments and to acquire the basic necessities for a new baby. Maram's isolation compounded the anxieties she felt at being separated from her husband. She was unhappy that her husband wasn't there to support her and also concerned about her children, for whom the social worker had arranged childcare while Maram was in hospital: 'I wasn't feeling happy about my husband, because I feel far from him. And I feel scared also. And stressed about my kids. Because I knew that they were okay [with] the babysitter, but some of my kids didn't eat when I wasn't there.'

She later repeated: 'I was scared about my kids. Because I was thinking all the time about my kids. And because I was alone, and my husband wasn't there. So he could not keep my kids.'

Maram gave birth at 2 am and left the hospital at 5 pm the same day. In her interview, she said she lied to hospital staff about feeling poorly because she was so concerned about her other children and wanted to get home to them as soon as possible:

> When I wanted to go, the doctors tell me that my baby is okay and he has no problems. She asked me if I feel okay to go, because I asked her to go. I remember I was lying to the doctor, because I was thinking about my kids. So I told her that I feel okay, and I'm fine, and I want to go to my home. So she let me.

Upon returning home, Maram was too ill to look after all of her children, but was able to call a friend from another city to stay with her for the day. Afterwards, Maram felt well enough to care for her children by herself, although she made it clear that this was very difficult for her:

Gwyneth:　　　　　So once your friend went home, where else did you get help or support?

Maram　　　　　Okay. She said, 'I didn't get support from anybody, [through　　　　　but I don't have a choice. I need to wake[?] for interpreter]:　　　　　my kids.'

It was clear in our interview that Maram was still very distressed by how difficult the weeks after giving birth had been, but felt she had 'no choice' in the absence of any other support. Her husband was eventually able to make it to the UK and reunite with his family.

Bordering processes and the stratification of extended family support

The privileging of the heteronormative nuclear family in bordering processes stratifies support available from extended family networks during pregnancy, childbirth, and new motherhood. Many Global North countries offer, at best, limited opportunities to sponsor parents, siblings, or other extended family members for entry and settlement (Strasser et al, 2009; Bragg and Wong, 2016); in the UK, with rare exceptions, only spouses and children can be sponsored on family visas. This prevents extended family members from moving to the country to provide support with reproductive tasks. Studies of the effects of family bordering legislation in Europe and Canada have documented the extra burden this stratified reproduction places on migrant women, particularly in juggling paid work with unpaid mothering responsibilities (Strasser et al, 2009; Bragg and Wong, 2016). This is further compounded, in the UK, by a visitors' visa system designed to maximize the economic benefits of tourism and filter out potential overstayers, based on a classist and racist construction of countries of the Global South as innately less desirable places to live. As of 2024, citizens of most wealthy, predominantly white countries, including within the EU and North America, were able to visit the UK for up to 6 months without requiring a visa (UK Visas and Immigration, 2024), while citizens of other countries might have to pay hefty fees and negotiate bureaucratic hurdles, or might simply be refused entry to the country (Gov-uk, n.d.-d).

For those of my participants whose mothers, especially, were able to visit, they were an important source of practical and emotional support. Edyta, who is from Eastern Europe, mentioned that both her parents provided practical support in the early days of motherhood, allowing her to focus on caring for her new baby: 'After I left hospital, my dad arrived. And after that, my mum. So we had visitors all the time. And they were helping out with cleaning, they were helping.'

Teresa is from South East Asia, and her parents came to visit for 5 months because, in her words, 'the maximum time you can stay here on a visitor visa is 6 months'. In her interview, Teresa discussed the importance of her mother's support when it came to breastfeeding:

> Because it was already stressful enough to be breastfeeding. Because it was a hard ... it was really hard as well to get into that. If my mum wasn't here, I probably wouldn't have persisted with the breastfeeding, because she was the only one who was telling me every day, 'Keep

doing it every day. If it hurts, the more you have to keep doing it. Because it gets better.'

Asra is from South Asia, and was initially concerned that her mother would not be able to visit because she was having difficulties with her passport. These were resolved, however, and she was able to visit for the birth of Asra's child, and for a period afterwards: 'Thankfully she was here and that helped a lot because of course after I gave birth, I did not have to care about anything about other than my own baby, the rest of it she took care of, yeah.'

However, for other participants, the bureaucracy associated with getting a visitor's visa posed an insurmountable obstacle. Anoush's experience demonstrates both the way in which the complexities of the visa system can serve as a barrier to visits from extended family and the emotional distress this can cause. She is from a Middle Eastern country and went to visit her mother in that country while pregnant, and again a few months after giving birth. She indicated that this seemed easier than trying to get a visa for her mother to come visit:

> But I didn't do that because here in the UK it's the law, she can come, but sometimes you found some … more information, they need more information. And I will speak to the lawyer and he told me 'we need a lot of paper', and my mum is not young to do that. But they need some papers to go there and something translation and all of this takes time.

Anoush also discussed how much she missed her mother during her pregnancy:

> Sometimes I feel worried because I feel alone, my husband works full time and I have my son stay with me, he didn't go to nursery in this time. And just stay and clean or tidy my house and cooking as well. But I remember the first three months in my second pregnancy, I am not feeling good. Maybe just because I stayed alone, not with my mum, because for the first pregnancy I stayed with her, and she brought everything for me. So the second one was more difficult for me than the first.

Two groups of my participants were absolutely unable to have their extended families visit, in both cases because they would have been considered possible overstayers. The first was women from a country embroiled in conflict, notably Syria and Libya.[5] Strikingly, visitors' visas were denied even when the family members in question were living in safe third countries, including in North America and Europe. Sally is from Syria, and is a refugee living in the UK. She had wanted her mother, who lives in Canada, to come for a visit but the visa application was denied:

> I kind of expected it … yeah, because it's hard to get a visa anyways, to the UK, so … you can tell if she's coming from Syria, and – although she was coming from Canada, she had the visa in Canada, and I thought this is going to support her application. But … they said they didn't have enough evidence that she's going to leave …

The second group of women whose family members could not visit were asylum seekers. In a text message following up on her interview, for example, Sana indicated that while she was not in touch with her family in her country of origin, she was in touch with her husband's family, but that there was no way for her mother-in-law to come and visit because she and her husband are asylum seekers.

Several of the women I interviewed fell into one or both groups. As with Sana, it was clear that they missed the support provided by family. Biba, who is from Libya, discussed how much she missed having female family members around, although she felt she had come through the experience stronger:

> In Libya, your mother, your sisters and your friends. When you go to a country when you don't know anyone and you have a baby, you kind of feel responsible about everything, because no one comes to help you. You have to leave the house and you have to, everything, you have to do it by your own. So, I learned a lot. It was a good experience, it was hard, but I learned a lot.

However, it was not just the support that was missed; there was an emotional toll at being separated from one's family during a major life event. Family practices are critical to making a home; as discussed earlier, the state's refusal to recognize or respect family ties sends a message that one is 'less-than' and outside the national home. Rana is from Libya and is a dependent on her husband's visa. In her interview, she mentioned that 'due to all the difficulty of obtaining the visa', her family was unable to come and visit her. When I asked her if she thought being an immigrant had made any difference to her experience of being pregnant in the UK, she said: 'The experience, I've got two experience. One good experience, one bad experience. The good experience is the care and the treatment I received in this country, is perfect. And the bad experience is, my family are not around me.'

She later added: 'I wish, this is one of the points I was actually making, if the government, you know, give authorization to, for example our family. Our parents to come to visit us in this situation. When a woman gives birth.'

Lames, who is also from Syria and is in the UK on a spousal visa, explicitly drew the connection between having one's family ties respected and full citizenship in her interview. She said:

> Being without family is – my family can't come here, because they will be refused a visa. But they can't get visas, because they are Syrian. So they can't come here. And it was difficult to talk to them on the phone. And it's difficult. I never imagined that, when I got pregnant and gave birth, my mum would be far from me.

Lames' mother-in-law, who is also Syrian but lives in a European country, was similarly denied a visa: 'She was refused a visa because she's Syrian. So this adds to the experience, that you're a second-class citizen.'

Better Births, *'the family', and reproductive citizenship*

It is striking, then, that *Better Births* (National Maternity Review, 2016) constructs 'the family' as both the location of reproduction and a source of support, and suggests that reproductive decision-making must incorporate the wider family. As noted in Chapter 2, 'personalized care', the paradigm for the delivery of maternity services in England, is defined as care 'centred on the woman, her baby and *her family*, based around their needs and their decisions' (National Maternity Review, 2016: 8; emphasis added). *Better Births* also states that 'where appropriate [the birthing mother's] partner or family members should be involved' in drawing up her personalized care plan (44). Postnatal care is supposed to '[i]nvolve [the birthing woman's] partner, family and friends who will play a key part in supporting her to raise her child' (62). This centring of the family in plans around maternity services while bordering processes limit some migrants' access to their family, and even their partner, serves multiple functions. First, it reinforces the marginal status of migrants, and indeed citizens, affected by family bordering processes; the importance of family in pregnancy and childbirth is emphasized even as the family ties of pregnant migrants are disregarded. As noted previously, the non-recognition of family ties is a long-standing strategy for rendering individuals and groups abject. Second, as I discuss in more depth in Chapter 5, *Better Births* can be read as constructing an 'ideal birthing citizen', the person who 'should' be reproducing the nation state. The presumption of family involvement excludes some migrant women from that norm. Third, and related to this, the presumption of family support may influence the provision of maternity care, negatively affecting birthing people who are separated from their family. However, some midwives, like Ines' (discussed later), may be aware of the particular challenges facing migrant patients separated from their families, and offer support.

It takes a (transnational) village – even if you have to build it yourself

My participants were not passive in the face of the reproductive injustice and stratification produced by family bordering processes. Ayetree and Emily both showed resourcefulness and determination in negotiating bordering processes when making decisions around reproduction. Furthermore, as I now discuss, many of my participants sought out and organized alternate sources and networks of support. While these activities did not directly contest bordering processes and resultant reproductive injustice, they can be read as examples of what Katz (2004) refers to as 'resilience', in that they allowed my participants to sustain themselves under oppressive social forces. Katz (2004) distinguishes 'resilience' from 'reworking', the redistribution or reconstitution of resources to address social problems, and 'resistance', involving direct challenges to 'specific conditions of oppression and exploitation at various scales' (251). Katz's (2004) framework is useful in that it allows an appreciation and analysis of multiple forms of agency, while not overstating the existence of direct and explicit contestation.[6]

Furthermore, drawing on De Genova (2010b), these acts of 'resilience' can be read as posing an *implied* challenge to bordering processes, which is consistent with Katz's (2004) wider conceptualization of these 'categories' of agency as fluid and overlapping. De Genova (2010b) has noted the parallels between the queer activist slogan 'We're here, we're queer, get used to it!' and the slogan shouted by undocumented migrants at protests across the US in 2006: 'Here we are and we're not leaving.' In both cases, De Genova points out, activists are not making demands of the government; instead, they are asserting, unapologetically, their presence, their already–existing status as members of the community. Given the significance of women's reproductive practices to the continuity of the nation state, I would argue my participants' activities to alleviate the stratified reproduction to which they are subject should be viewed in a similar light. While some of my participants may leave the UK, whether to return to their countries of origin or to move to a different country, many intend to stay. In short, regardless of state recognition of their family forms, they *are* reproducing the next generation of British citizens (even when their children do not have formal citizenship), and they are seeking out the resources they need to do so.

Transnational communication and family support for reproduction

Many of my participants discussed being supported by their family, and sharing in the joy and excitement of a new baby, through the use of transnational communication technologies. This was true both of participants whose families were able to visit, but were not able to be present for the entire pregnancy, and those who were not. They were thus able to maintain relationships with, and access support from, a broader family formation than the heteronormative nuclear ideal underpinning UK bordering processes and discourses and policies around citizenship. There is an extensive literature on the use of communication technologies to maintain transnational family ties, and the complexities and unevenness this can produce in relationships (Parreñas, 2014; Francisco, 2015). Nonetheless, those of my participants on good terms with their families overseas tended to discuss them as an important source of both practical advice and emotional reassurance, particularly valued when dealing with a major life event in a new country. Biba discussed in her interview feeling scared during her C-section and wanting to talk with her mum, and the medical staff reassuring her that she was allowed to use her phone:

> I told [labour ward staff] I am feeling a bit scared now when I'm in an operation, can I use my phone? So, they looked at each and other and yeah, who is going to talk to you now? I told them, I want to talk to my mum. They laughed and they said okay. It was very nice.

She then explained that during the operation, and her stay in hospital, she used Facebook Messenger to chat with both her mother and mother-in-law: 'Yeah, actually I chatted with her. Not by voice or video, I just chatted with her. Like in the hospital. I was chatting with my mum and my mother-in-law. They both were chatting with me.'

Amara, who is also from Libya, talked about the reassurance provided by her family overseas, especially with regard to her anxieties about being pregnant and giving birth in a new country: 'Yes, I was actually supported by my family by Viber, we used to use Viber to talk and they were always there to support me and encourage me to calm down and to cope with the situation.'

She continued: 'For example, they were always giving me examples about other Libyan ladies who came to the UK and gave birth, and they were always telling me that they always with you, even if we are not around, they are always around.'

Building local networks of support

Additionally, many of the women I interviewed were able to establish networks of support in the UK, made up of in-laws and/or friends. Some of the women I interviewed reported having good relations with their in-laws who lived in the UK, and their mother- and sisters-in-law especially as providing the kind of support they would have gotten from their own family, had that family been in the UK. Aisha, who is from the Middle

East and in the UK on a spousal visa, was accompanied in the labour ward by her husband and sister-in-law, and described her sister-in-law as having done a 'great job' helping her. Ayetree was advised by her mother-in-law, a massage therapist, about how to best deal with her pelvic girdle pain; this was useful because she did not find the NHS group physiotherapy classes she had been enrolled in helpful.

Several of the women described making friends in asylum accommodation, through places of worship, in migrant support groups, through ethnic community networks, and with their neighbours, and that these friends stepped in and provided the sort of support they might have gotten from family members. Leila, a refugee from the Middle East, was active in a refugee support group and described the help that other members provided her with when she was pregnant: 'And during my pregnancy, I had care from my friends, actually, and they made a group for me. Only for cooking. So I didn't cook for a month.'

Sally stated in her interview that she had a 'good community of friends' who provided her with practical support:

> Well, really a lot, [my friends] came, they … they helped me give her a bath, the first bath. They helped me, they … they cooked for us. So maybe for two or three weeks I didn't cook myself, they cooked for us. They came for like visit, support, staying around … they offer gifts as well. It's not this actually, you just want them to be there … Yeah. What else did they do? They give you like things that they used like high chairs, and things that they don't need for… for that time, and they support you with stuff as well. So I didn't buy a high chair, I didn't buy the pump, they give me an electric pump. They gave me so many things, they help – yeah, they were there for so many things really.

She explained how she had come to make these friends: 'So parts of these people, I know from the mosque… Part of them is a Syrian community, so we know each other from each other – so if you know a friend she will introduce you to other people, and then you get a bigger community.'

Zahra had been reunited in the UK with a friend from her country of origin, and had been incorporated into a wider social network through this friend. She described the support her friends gave (as related by the interpreter, who is referring to Zahra in the third person):

> She said when she used to have an appointment with the midwife or anything, they used to care about her children, look after her children, and all the time they used to bring her food, when she got the baby, until 15 days, just every day, one of them bring food for her, support her, come and clean and do the housework and look after the children.

Finally, some of the women I interviewed mentioned their midwife as an important source of emotional support. As I discuss more in Chapter 4, midwives who are aware of the challenges facing pregnant migrants can be invaluable in negotiating bordering processes and the reproductive stratification they produce. Ines, who is from Libya, described the following conversation with her midwife:

> I felt treated very special. And she was always there for me, and she even said it: '*Don't think that because you are alone in this country and your family they are not around you and you don't have a female support from your family … I am here for you*, and if you need me any time, you can call me any time. And don't feel worried or feel that because you are alone may something gonna happen to you. We are here for you and we stand by you.' (Emphasis added)

Ines' midwife clearly understood that she would have been used to a wider network of family support during pregnancy and childbirth, and did her best to fill that gap.

Conclusion

Family bordering processes both reflect and reinforce the association of a particular family model – in the case of the UK, the white, heteronormative, patriarchal, economically productive nuclear family – with citizenship. Both migrants and citizens may be disciplined by these processes into doing family 'correctly', for example, by preventing people from living with their spouse in the UK unless they can demonstrate economic productivity. Concurrently, having one's family ties recognized and respected is a marker of citizenship and belonging, and the conditionality attached to this recognition contributes to the production of citizenship as hierarchical and multi-tiered. Because the family is also the site of the reproduction of the nation state, family bordering processes are informed by anxieties around reproduction, and also serve to discipline the reproductive practices of both migrants and citizens. These processes place significant constraints on migrant women's reproductive autonomy, and differentially distribute both state and family support for reproduction. This shaped my participants' experiences of reproductive decision-making, pregnancy, childbirth, and new motherhood. These experiences were further stratified according to the social location of the women in question and the resources available to them.

However, the women with whom I worked were not passive in the face of these constraints. They demonstrated tremendous 'resilience' (Katz, 2004), negotiating family bordering processes as best they could in their family planning decisions; maintaining extended transnational family networks, on whom they could rely for support and advice, with communication technologies; and forming new networks of support in the UK. In doing so, they asserted their presence as individuals who *are* building a family life in the UK, regardless of state anxieties regarding their suitability and the denial of their family ties. The activities of individuals and groups offering support to migrant women should similarly be read as acts of 'resilience'. The material and emotional support offered helped my participants sustain their reproductive work despite the injustice and stratification produced by family bordering processes. These actors can additionally be understood as offering an implied challenge to bordering processes and associated discourses that devalue migrant family forms, and therefore as potentially contributing to wider struggles for reproductive justice.

Chapter 4 considers a different dimension of stratified reproduction produced by bordering processes, exploring how policies and processes differentially distributing access to social citizenship impacted my participants' access to NHS maternity care. Multiple bordering processes around different services associated with social citizenship – including the NHS, but also housing, benefits, and access to the labour market – overlap and interact with each other, as well as with gendered, racialized, and classed discourses of citizenship, and the individual situation of my participants, to form a complex matrix of reproductive stratification.

4

Social Citizenship, Proliferating Borders, and Stratified Reproduction

Introduction

In this chapter, I explore how bordering processes operating within and through the sites, services, and resources associated with social citizenship serve as instruments of stratified reproduction, especially with regard to NHS maternity care. As discussed in Chapter 1, concerns about the national reproductive future play a key role in structuring social citizenship, and in turn, the services and resources associated with social citizenship, and their design and distribution (which often reflect and reinforce hierarchical and multi-tiered understandings of citizenship), serve to shape and discipline the reproductive practices of citizens and non-citizens. Social citizenship, therefore, serves as an instrument of reproductive stratification, differently valuing and supporting the reproductive choices and practices of different individuals and groups.

Bordering processes have long operated through social citizenship, differentially distributing resources and services associated with the welfare state to non-citizens depending on their immigration status and social location, and in doing so, reflecting and reinforcing discourses around citizenship and belonging, and disciplining migrants' behaviour. This further stratifies reproduction, as migrants have different degrees of access to services and resources necessary for pregnancy, childbirth, and parenthood. The multiplication and proliferation of bordering processes has both entrenched and diversified this stratification, as the reach of the state into the reproductive practices of migrants has expanded and strengthened. However, bordering processes are *situated*, and the proliferation of these processes has also opened new spaces for resistance, as they come into contact with the ideologies and practices associated with different bordering sites. With regard to NHS maternity services, the professional commitments of some midwives has led to them undermining or resisting attempts to restrict access to services. Reproductive stratification produced by NHS bordering may be thus further variegated according to the perspectives and practices of individual midwives.

Moreover, as outlined in Chapter 1, the reproductive justice framework highlights the way in which interacting sets of discourses and policy regimes constrain reproductive autonomy, pointing to the importance of a holistic analytical approach. Applying this insight to the relationship between bordering and reproduction reveals how proliferating bordering processes overlap and interact, sometimes reinforcing, and sometimes mitigating, each other. Bordering processes that limit migrants' access to income and adequate housing stratify reproduction because both money and housing are necessary for a healthy pregnancy, safe birth, and new parenthood. Additionally, they also interact with discourses and practices around NHS maternity care to reinforce NHS bordering and further stratify access to these services. At the same time, however, the interaction between bordering around income and housing, and NHS bordering, means that the former may also be mitigated by the specificities of the NHS as a bordering site, in particular, the construction of some pregnant migrants as especially deserving of extra support.

I begin this chapter by reviewing how bordering processes operate through social citizenship, and the potential implications for stratified reproduction. I then look at the NHS bordering regime as an instrument of stratified reproduction, exploring how this was experienced by my participants, but also how the professional and ethical commitments of NHS clinical staff served, at times, to mitigate and undermine this stratification. This is followed by a discussion of how bordering processes limit some migrants' access to resources – namely a sufficient income and adequate housing – necessary for a safe and healthy pregnancy and new motherhood, and how this additionally serves to further stratify access to NHS maternity services. This stratification is, however, also variegated by discourses and practices associated with maternity services, including contested notions of 'deservingness'; the interpellation of pregnant women as 'good choosers' in *Better Births* (National Maternity Review, 2016); and the professional commitments of NHS clinical staff. The quasi-ubiquity of bordering processes expands the state's power to stratify reproduction and limit, through multiple vectors, precarious migrants' access to critical medical care; yet, this ubiquity also means that there are multiple points and sites at which bordering processes may be mitigated or undermined by site-specific philosophies and practices.

Bordering social citizenship

Discourses, policies, and practices associated with social citizenship serve as instruments of reproductive stratification, differentially distributing material, discursive, and cultural support for reproduction and reproductive autonomy according to wider discourses around reproduction and national belonging. As I explored in Chapter 1, citizenship and reproduction are mutually constitutive, and this is visible with regard to social citizenship. Concerns about the national reproductive future play a key role in structuring social citizenship, and in turn, the services and resources associated with social citizenship, and their design and distribution, serve to shape and discipline the reproductive practices of citizens and non-citizens. The state differently allocates resources for reproduction depending on the social location of individuals and groups and whether they are constructed as capable of reproducing the nation state 'correctly'. In both the US and the UK, discourses calling on citizens to reproduce 'responsibly' by only having as many children as they can 'afford' are materialized in policies capping benefit payments to families after a certain number of children (Solinger 2001; Gov.uk, 2021; see also Chapter 1). Additionally, policies and services associated with social citizenship shape who is considered responsible for different reproductive tasks and how these tasks should be undertaken. I have previously discussed, for example, how the post-war UK welfare state was premised on the assumption that reproductive tasks would largely be carried out by women, within the home.

The stratified reproduction produced by social citizenship is further compounded and variegated by bordering policies and practices that are informed by anxieties around the reproduction of the nation state and differentially distribute access to associated services and entitlements according to immigration status. Critically, social citizenship has long been central to bordering processes. Restricting migrants' access to social citizenship helps to reinforce the symbolic boundary between migrants and citizens, even as the entitlements of social citizenship are becoming increasingly eroded and conditional under neoliberal restructuring (Tyler, 2013). Furthermore, differential access to various aspects of social citizenship is central to the construction of different immigration categories. In the UK, for example, people on work visas are unable to collect most benefits and are expected to stay in employment; asylum seekers, by contrast, are not allowed to work and are also excluded from the mainstream benefits system, supported instead through parallel asylum support. This can also serve to indicate which migrants are considered more 'desirable' than others; within the EU, migrants from other EU countries are generally able to access welfare state services on far more favourable terms than third country nationals, sending a message about who is more welcome. Limiting migrants' access to the welfare state also has a disciplinary function, indicating what behaviour is expected of both migrants and citizens – namely, economic self-sufficiency congruent with neoliberal models of citizenship – and producing this behaviour in migrants (Anderson, 2013).

All of this has significant repercussions for stratified reproduction. Discourses constructing different groups of migrants as more or less threatening to the national reproductive future are materialized in policies differentially distributing resources necessary for reproduction, and disciplining migrants' reproductive activities accordingly. As noted previously, No Recourse to Public Funds (NRPF) policies require that migrants on spousal and work visas, who may one day be citizens, demonstrate 'responsible reproductive citizenship' by having children without support from the state. By contrast, asylum seekers, who are seen as particularly undesirable, are forbidden from working, provided with minimal financial support, and housed in substandard conditions (all of which I discuss in more detail later in this chapter), and thus arguably sent a message that they should not be reproducing *at all* (Lonergan, 2018).

The role of bordering processes around social citizenship in creating stratified reproduction is further complicated and reconfigured by the proliferation and multiplication of these processes, and their expansion into the spaces of everyday life. This proliferation of the border means that the influence of the state on the reproductive practices and reproductive autonomy of migrants has both expanded and strengthened. Furthermore, as noted in Chapter 1, bordering processes are situated in that they impact people differently depending on their location within hierarchical and multi-tiered discourses around citizenship, and also, in the sense that they are shaped by the practices and philosophies associated with different bordering sites. These practices and philosophies may be congruent with state agendas around the disciplining of migrants' reproductive practices, but they may also challenge or oppose state agendas. Thus, pregnant migrants and new mothers may now encounter varying iterations of bordering processes and practices at multiple sites, and these iterations interact and overlap with each other and may reinforce or mitigate each other.

Stratified reproduction and the NHS charging regime

Policies and processes governing migrants' access to NHS maternity services are among the most visible causes of stratified reproduction experienced by pregnant and birthing migrants. They exclude some migrants, depending on their immigration status, from free necessary medical care, and may be a source of anxiety for others, regardless of their statutory entitlements. This stratification may be aggravated by overzealous gatekeepers, whose implementation of these processes is shaped by discourses and practices around citizenship and bordering that construct migrants, especially racially minoritized migrants, as burdening the NHS (see Chapter 2). However, these bordering processes may also be mitigated by the professional and ethical commitments of individual NHS maternity staff – a consequence of the specificities of NHS maternity services as a bordering site. Finally, pregnant and birthing migrants themselves may contest exclusion from maternity services, further stratifying reproduction according to the resources and support available to these migrants.

At present in the UK, migrants with Indefinite Leave to Remain can access NHS secondary care, including maternity care, on the same terms as UK citizens, as can refugees and asylum seekers with an active application or appeal. Migrants on visas that allow them to stay in the UK for more than 6 months, including work, family, and student visas, must pay the Immigration Health Surcharge, and can then access most NHS services free at the point of delivery. Migrants on short-term visas, visitors, 'failed' asylum seekers, and undocumented migrants are all required to pay for NHS secondary care, including maternity care, at 150 per cent of the cost of the care, unless they are covered by an international healthcare agreement (such as the European Health Insurance Card) (Department of Health and Social Care, 2024). Maternity care, including antenatal and postnatal care, is deemed to be always 'immediately necessary', and patients can only be charged afterwards (Department of Health and Social Care, 2024: 5). However, as I elaborate upon later, the prospect of debt still has a deterrent effect upon patients, and an outstanding debt of more than £500 to the NHS may result in future visa applications being denied (Home Office, 2023). Additionally, there are 'humanitarian exemptions' for certain categories of people, including trafficked persons, or if the healthcare being sought is to address the effects of rape or domestic violence (Department of Health and Social Care, 2024).

The charging regime has significant material consequences for pregnant migrants. Research suggests that fear of being charged leads some precarious pregnant migrants, including those who might be eligible for free NHS secondary care, to delay seeking out antenatal care (Shortall et al, 2015; Feldman, 2017; 2021; Nellums et al, 2021). The 2019 MBRRACE-UK report into maternal deaths and morbidity in the UK from 2015 to 2017 raised the possibility that NHS charging was dissuading some pregnant migrants from seeking antenatal care, and linked the policy to three maternal deaths (Knight et al, 2019: 28). These concerns were raised by some of my participants as well. Joanne, a midwife in Greater Manchester, reported that some migrant patients were delaying seeking out antenatal care because of fears that they would be charged. This was echoed by Annie, who works in the third sector supporting migrants:

> So at this point, they often, we're told by women that they've been told they're going to be charged over £7000 for their care, and they've decided, or they're thinking about not attending antenatal appointments, and wanting to know if they don't attend … if they

reduce the number of appointments they attend, will that reduce the cost of the care?

Huda, another third sector worker, reported: 'The woman said that "I didn't want to go to my appointments in the hospital, because I knew I was going to be charged".'

The stratified reproduction produced by the NHS charging regime may be further exacerbated by the 'mistakes' made by gatekeepers regarding who is entitled to free maternity care. There is significant evidence in the wider literature that it is not unusual for Overseas Visitors Officers (OVOs) and other gatekeepers to wrongly prevent migrants from accessing NHS secondary care to which they are entitled; this may include a failure to identify patients who qualify for a humanitarian exemption (discussed earlier) (Feldman, 2017; 2021; Nellums et al, 2021). These regular 'errors' should be understood as reflecting the discourses and practices of bordering processes within and outside the NHS. NHS staff, both clinical and non-clinical, may now be expected to undertake bordering work as part of their responsibilities (Cassidy, 2018). Given the complexity of immigration policy in general, and of that specifically dealing with entitlement to free NHS secondary care, it is not surprising that regular mistakes occur. Moreover, it can be argued that current policy encourages NHS staff to take a 'paranoid view' when determining eligibility for secondary care, as trusts can be fined for *not* charging a patient, but not for *wrongly* charging a patient (Department of Health, 2014). Indeed, trusts can charge eligible patients 150 per cent of the standard tariff for any care provided, a potentially important source of income during the current funding crisis (Department of Health, 2014: see Chapter 2). Furthermore, racialized discourses and practices around citizenship and immigration may inform gatekeeper decisions around charging. Although the OVOs I interviewed insisted that they did not racially profile patients when making decisions about entitlement to free care, the Institute for Public Policy Research (Morris and Nanda, 2021) suggests that racial profiling *is* used by some NHS gatekeepers. This was also echoed by Annie:

> Black women who are British or who are exempt because they have indefinite leave to remain tell us that they feel they are subject to racism by the Overseas Visitor Team. And the way they're being questioned about their nationality, their immigration status, and the presumption that they would be charged, in a way that we never hear from white women.

During the end-of-project workshop, migrant participants made it clear that they experienced the charging regime as racist.

All of the migrant women I interviewed, except one, had a visa status that permitted them NHS maternity care free of charge at the point of delivery. However, three of the women I interviewed, Jade, Asra, and Humaira, were erroneously told they might have to pay for maternity care. All three women are racially minoritized, although I do not know exactly how this factored into the errors being made. Additionally, two of my participants stated that their GP had asked them about their immigration status, even though primary care is free of charge to all residents of the UK, regardless of their visa. Amal, an African woman in the UK on a spousal visa, stated in her interview that her GP asked about her papers when she first registered; Emily, a white North American woman, who lived in London before moving to the north of England, also reported that when she first registered for a GP in London, she was asked for her visa. Research by the charity Doctors of the World found that un(der)documented migrants were being refused registry with GPs, suggesting that Emily and Amal's experiences are not unique (Shortall et al, 2015).

These 'mistakes' by gatekeepers are obviously harmful, potentially denying pregnant migrants necessary medical care. Even where the mistakes are resolved, as they were for my participants, they can cause significant stress (see also Nellums et al, 2021). Asra, for example, stated:

> Actually, because, I mean I was pretty confident that I was eligible for it, but you know, when you are told like this, so I was like, I was little scared for some time that if I do not, I have to end up paying for it, I mean that would be a huge amount probably so I had this thought in my mind that, oh, should I go back to India then?

Similarly, Julia, a GP who works with migrants, related the story of a woman who had experienced severe trauma in her country of origin and needed extra support when giving birth in the UK:

> And then she was billed seven thousand pounds and obviously had no means to pay that and then was getting these awful phone calls from debt collectors and letters through saying it would impact her immigration status if she didn't pay and really scary, created a whole lot of anxiety.

The bill was eventually cancelled, but it took over a year.

As suggested by Asra and Julia's experiences, the charging regime further stratifies reproduction according to whether the people being charged for care, correctly or not, have the knowledge, resources, and experience to advocate for themselves, or failing that, support from a knowledgeable third party. Asra, who came to the UK as a dependent upon her husband's work visa, said that she was 'a little scared, but not too much' because she was confident she was eligible for free care. She was able to establish her entitlement to NHS care, but had to navigate what sounds like a complex bureaucratic process to do so:

> So I had to contact, it's called [redacted email address]. Yeah, and there was this NHS eligibility form. I think I first called them up and then they told me because on the phone I had the email ID as well, so they told me to send these documents and then I emailed them on this email ID, and then so, I emailed them on 30th January and yeah, the next day as well, they were like I confirm that you are eligible for the free NHS.

Jade, a refugee, received a letter from her maternity hospital, shortly before she was due to give birth, telling her she was expected to pay for care. She made it clear that she found it stressful but also that she was confident she could resolve the situation: 'And I was like what?! So two weeks before like are you joking [laughs] but then because I knew it was a mistake… Anyway I just rang them and – I emailed back actually with the evidence that I wasn't – I wasn't meant to pay.'

Both Jade and Asra are well-educated and speak fluent English, and both understood the British immigration system enough to know that they were entitled to free NHS care. Julia was able to advocate for her patient, adding: 'I think [pregnant migrants are] often charged erroneously and the times I've challenged it, I've usually been successful cause it's usually been some kind of mistake made about what's gone on.'

However, many people asked to pay for NHS maternity care will have neither the personal resources nor the social support to contest these charges.

NHS bordering and contesting discourses of 'deservingness' and care

NHS maternity services as a bordering site are also shaped by NHS clinical staff's understanding of their own role, their professional commitments, and their perception of pregnant migrants. An emerging literature has documented that healthcare workers' perceptions of the 'deservingness' of precarious migrants can shape whether these migrants can access medical care, and their experience of this care, regardless of their legal entitlements (Willen, 2012; Willen and Cook, 2016; Sahraoui, 2020a; 2021). Furthermore, as Malakasis and Sahraoui (2020: 169) point out, 'pregnant women are differently positioned on the moral map of migrants' health-related deservingness, due to their status as women and future mothers'. On the one hand, pregnant migrants may be seen as especially *undeserving* because they are introducing a 'foreign' population into the nation state and may potentially be trying to build a home where they are unwanted (Willen and Cook, 2016). On the other hand, the perceived vulnerability of pregnant migrants may cause them to be seen as especially *deserving*; this may be particularly true of asylum seekers and refugees if they are understood to be in the receiving country through circumstances beyond their control (Sahraoui, 2021).

The impact of NHS bordering on pregnant migrants may therefore be reinforced or mitigated by the actions of NHS staff, further variegating the resultant stratified reproduction. As I elaborate upon in Chapter 5, there is extensive evidence that racially minoritized women are subject to prejudice and racism from individual NHS staff when seeking maternity care (Jomeen and Redshaw, 2013; Garcia et al, 2015; Firdous et al, 2020; Birthrights, 2022; Peter et al, 2022). Some NHS clinical staff may also internalize discourses constructing (racially minoritized) migrants as a burden on the NHS. Marie, for example, trains NHS staff as part of her work, and suggested that her experiences were mixed:

> [O]n the whole it's mostly great, they're there because they want to understand someone's rights out there. And they get very confused about immigration. And why wouldn't they? Because it's so complicated, the system … But I have heard what I'd call sort of Daily Mail-y comments about scarce services being taken by people deliberately just coming here to have children and whatever, yeah.

Nonetheless, most of the NHS clinical staff I interviewed expressed opposition to charging pregnant migrants for maternity care, arguing that it conflicted with their professional commitments and/or philosophical beliefs regarding healthcare as a human right (see also Feldman et al, 2019). Joanne, for example, stated:

> I think it's a basic human right to have access to healthcare, so… having a child is a part of that process. Of course if you are going round doing something that you shouldn't be doing and then you've got poorly as a result of it, people might think should you be charged for it? But I just think access to good healthcare is part of your human rights.

Consequently, many of the clinical staff I interviewed took steps to undermine the NHS bordering regime, or at least minimize its impact. As outlined in Chapter 3, these kind of activities may not involve overtly contesting current NHS bordering regimes, but they can be read as acts of 'resilience' and/or 'reworking' (Katz, 2004), allowing pregnant migrants to sustain their reproductive work under oppressive conditions and re-allocating resources to support them. The activities can also be read as implicitly challenging discourses devaluing the lives and health of pregnant migrants. Some suggested it was 'not their job' to record the immigration status or chargeability of patients. Rosa, an anaesthetist, for example, said:

> I'm very happy not to establish that. I'll establish it in the sense of whether it affects their healthcare, and I will probably try and write it down in a way that is clear the ways in which it affects the healthcare, but I will tactically not write down the fact they are not ordinarily resident if I think that's what's going on. I try to really restrict my clinical notes and stuff to be focused on the medical care.

Noor, a midwife working in Greater Manchester, similarly said that she 'forgot' to ask when treating patients and that there was 'always a way' to avoid making a note of a patient's eligibility. A few staff also discussed intervening with the Overseas Visitors Office to help patients who were being charged. Ruth, a community midwife, said in her interview that, if specifically asked by the OVOs whether a patient was chargeable:

> I will inform them, but there is also a letter that can be sent to them, to the Trust, to say 'this person has no means of paying, they will pay 1p a month or 2p a month'. And that letter goes in, and that tends to deal with the situation.

This means that the patient in question has a 'payment plan' and the Home Office will not be notified of their debt. The stratified reproduction produced by NHS bordering processes is thus further complicated by the *situatedness* of these processes, and the attitudes and actions of individual NHS staff.

Bordering processes and access to income and housing

Bordering processes located at other sites associated with social citizenship similarly stratify reproduction by differentially distributing access to the resources needed for safe and healthy pregnancies and to parent newborn babies. The following section focuses on two key themes that emerged during interviews with migrant women and third sector staff: poverty and housing. Bordering processes limited many of my participants' access to state benefits, and additionally prevented some, notably asylum seekers, from engaging with the labour market. Similarly, some of my participants were unable to access state support with housing, while the asylum-seeking participants were subject to dispersal and required to live in designated housing that was often inadequate. The stratified reproduction produced by the proliferation of bordering processes to various sites of social citizenship was highly variegated, interacting with the personal circumstances of migrants, including their immigration status, and their location within wider racialized, gendered, and classed discourses of citizenship and belonging; the attitudes and perceptions of gatekeepers; and the availability of alternate support.

Bordering processes producing poverty

As previously discussed, differential access to the means to support oneself is central to the construction of different immigration 'categories', and indicates which migrants are seen as more 'desirable' than others, as well as what behaviour is expected of migrants hoping to settle in the UK. Migrants on student, family, and work visas are expected to be financially self-sufficient and have NRPF, meaning they cannot access most benefits, including universal credit or child benefit. They can, however, access contributory benefits if they have paid in; these include Statutory Maternity Pay and Statutory Maternity Allowance (Home Office, 2014). Un(der) documented migrants are legally forbidden from working or accessing any benefits, and their deportable status renders them vulnerable to severe exploitation (De Genova, 2010a; Bloch, 2013). Asylum seekers are largely forbidden from working in the UK (Gower et al, 2022)[1] and instead are provided with housing and a basic financial stipend by the state. At the start of my fieldwork in late 2020, persons with open asylum claims were entitled to £37.75/week, increasing to £40.85/week by the end of the research project in 2022.[2] Pregnant women were entitled to an additional £3/week; babies under 1 year old, an additional £5/week; and children 1–3 years old an additional £3/week. Additionally, pregnant women were eligible for a one-off grant of £300 where their baby was due in 8 weeks or less, or was less than 6 weeks old. These payments have recently been increased and the eligibility for the one-off grant extended to 6 months old (Gov.uk, n.d.-a). 'Refused' asylum seekers can be made destitute, but may apply for support after 34 weeks of pregnancy (Gov.uk, n.d.-a).

The right to work legally, and a decently paid job (and/or a spouse in a decently paid job),[3] unsurprisingly emerged as a key fault line in the experience of stratified reproduction for my research participants. Some of my participants reported no major financial concerns with regards to supporting their family. Other migrant women I interviewed, however, experienced significant poverty while pregnant due to NRPF or having to live on asylum support. Julia, for example, discussed the problems posed by minimal asylum support for some of her patients:

> I think finances – living off five pound something a day, you know, is almost impossible isn't it? It's ridiculous. I think that, you know, it's not just living off five pounds a day for a week, it's living off five pounds a day for years and years and years. So you see people getting

into debt and you see people making, you know, really hard decisions about – about what they have and what their children have. In terms of antenatal care; obviously nutrition, you know, accessing food that you know and like and you can cook and have in. You know be[ing] able to maintain a healthy diet during the pregnancy is tricky.

Jill, who works in the third sector supporting asylum seekers and precarious migrants, discussed the poverty created by bordering processes as a challenge her organization tries to address:

I don't see the NRPF clients, but [other team members], they would see people like that that probably had young babies often, that found that maybe they were working, they got the No Recourse to Public Funds stipulation and they've had a baby. Or they're about to have a baby, and they're really worried, how on earth are they going to keep this job? Or how on earth are they gonna have enough money to look after them both?

Furthermore, several of my asylum-seeking participants in particular discussed relying on charities, or friends and family, for baby necessities. Maram, for example, explained in her interview that a volunteer from a local refugee support agency brought her clothing for her baby. Similarly, Lisa, an asylum seeker living in Greater Manchester, said in her interview that she had relied on a baby bank. Importantly, this kind of support is not available in all areas, and migrant women may not always have the awareness and connections to access this support. The personal circumstances and resources available to individual women can once again be seen to be interacting with border processes in stratifying reproduction.

As with the NHS charging regime, errors or hostility on the part of gatekeepers may further compound the poverty produced by bordering processes, denying migrants access to resources to which they are entitled. Jill discussed the process of securing support for her clients once they were 34 weeks pregnant, and the long delays in the Home Office's response, despite the urgent situation: 'I think the biggest frustration is the Home Office not responding to things. So we'll submit stuff, and you don't hear back for weeks. So we'll make an application for a maternity grant and spend our lives chasing it up.'

Humaira, who figures prominently in this chapter, was affected by a combination of bordering processes and bureaucratic error, further shaped by her social location as a migrant woman. Humaira was living in the UK on a spousal visa and pregnant with her third child when, with the support of her midwife, she made the decision to take her two children and leave her abusive husband. As noted in Chapter 3, the terms of spousal visas can trap women in abusive relationships (see Burman and Chantler, 2005; Anitha, 2008; Dudley, 2017), even with the policy changes that allow individuals in this situation to apply for Indefinite Leave to Remain in their own right, and to collect public funds through the Migrant Victims of Domestic Abuse Concession (which was the Destitution Domestic Violence Concession at the time Humaira needed support) (Home Office, 2024). After leaving her husband, Humaira went with her children to her local council office for support and was initially told, incorrectly, that she was not entitled to public funds. Although her social worker managed to resolve this for her, for several weeks afterwards, her British children's child benefit continued to be paid to her ex-husband, even though the children were living with her:

Gwyneth: Did the council or anyone give you any money while you were pregnant?

Humaira: Yeah. My social worker, she was giving every week. Yeah, money for my children. Basically, they were just paying for my children. ... You know, they were receiving benefit and it was going to my husband account. When I left the home, for three months, they paid to my husband. I told them, he's not living, but I don't know, they just took three months to proceed.

Housing, dispersal, and reproductive stratification

A similar pattern of complex stratification produced by the interaction of bordering processes with multiple social structures and the individual circumstances of migrants is visible with regard to accessing adequate housing, a clear necessity for a safe pregnancy and parenting a newborn baby. Access to housing is stratified, first, by immigration status. The Immigration Act 2014 requires landlords to check a prospective tenant's visa status to ensure they are legally resident in the UK, or face a fine if they are found to be letting to an un(der)documented migrant. In practice, this is further stratified according to racialized discourses around citizenship: a 'mystery shopper' exercise conducted by the Joint Council for the Welfare of Immigrants (2017) found that minority ethnic applicants without a British passport were more likely to be rejected by a landlord than white applicants without a British passport. Furthermore, as noted earlier, NRPF includes housing benefit, which means migrants on family, work, and student visas can find themselves at risk of homelessness. Pregnant migrants and those with children in this situation may be able to access housing under Section 17 of the Children Act 1989, which empowers local authorities to provide housing to 'children in need' regardless of NRPF (NRPF Network, n.d.); access to housing for impoverished migrants may thus be further stratified according to geographic location and the sympathies of the local authority.

Housing emerged as a concern for some of my more precarious participants, and for interviewees involved in supporting pregnant migrants (see also Lonergan, 2024a). As noted earlier, Humaira was initially (wrongly) told by her local council that she was not entitled to any support; after the intervention of her social worker, she was housed in a hotel. However, this housing was grossly inadequate, especially given that Humaira had two school age children to care for, including by ensuring they continued to attend school: 'I keep asking my social worker, please give me, maybe just a one-bedroom apartment where I have kitchen and I can do laundry. So, it was really, really hard. Every day, to wash clothes and dry them on the heating.'

In her interview, Humaira said she was very proud that she managed keep her two other children fed, clothed, and in school while living in these conditions. Similarly, Asmani explained how her NRPF status, in combination with caring responsibilities for her mother and daughter, meant she was forced to stay in her parents' overcrowded flat:

> So nine months was maternity allowance and but I lived with my parents and that's why I managed it all. And then nine months later we finished and then I can't go back to work and my mum's health issues are kind of no good … But it's still very, very hard time, and then because we did have only a two-bedroom flat, mum, dad, me, my daughter.

Asylum seekers are housed by the state on a no-choice basis and subject to 'dispersal', that is, being relocated, possibly multiple times, at short notice, potentially quite far from one's previous residence (Hynes, 2011; Darling, 2022). Asylum seekers are therefore not at risk of homelessness per se during their pregnancy, unless their claim is abruptly rejected; however, asylum housing is notoriously poor (Grayson, 2018; Darling, 2022). Marie described housing for pregnant asylum seekers in her interview:

> And that is pretty, pretty poor, inadequate, accommodation. And for pregnant women, I think the main issues are, is this … is the type of support they get, and when they get it, and how they get it. And for those in antenatal care, what we see is a lot of – and this has got much worse during Covid – a lot of women who are being housed in full-board accommodation. Pregnant women.

'Full-board' accommodation here refers to women being housed in a room in a house with meals provided, rather than being given their own flat. Sana was already pregnant with her third child when she and her husband, who were in the UK on student visas, decided to apply for asylum. She describes the initial accommodation they were forced to live in for part of her pregnancy:

> No, it's a big building, with so many rooms in there, like 150 rooms in there, like a very big building, just like a hotel or something. And we'd got a room, and everybody else got one room as well. So we've got a key for that, and there's a shared toilet that there was – there was not attached toilet at all, so we have to go to the … other toilet. But the condition of the shared accommodation was just terrible there. We … we lived nearly two, two and a half months there, and I kept requesting so many times, children were getting infections, I had an infection, and … it was terrible.

The role of bordering processes in excluding some pregnant migrants from housing was also further compounded by gatekeepers who were, at best, ill-informed and incompetent, and at worst, actively hostile. Elior, an asylum seeker, spent the Covid lockdown pregnant, with two children, in a one-bedroom flat, because the Home Office wrongly believed she only had one child; this had a significantly detrimental impact on her mental health. It required repeated phone calls to Migrant Help[4] to resolve the situation, and Elior described how the demeanour of their agents would range from friendly (while insisting Elior must be patient) to rude:

> Because you talk to the different … people. You find a … other one, you find the other ones will be very lovely, very understanding, they say okay maam, we understand your situation, you need to be patient, we already put this to our officer. And that was they talk to me [missed] [01:08:43] … bad mood, they would be like, we have given this to our officer, you need to be patient, wait! And take that tone. Yeah. So sometimes it feels like oh my goodness, no.

As discussed already, Humaira was repeatedly subject to errors on the part of gatekeepers. Moreover, while the local council eventually found more stable housing for Humaira and her family, she was told that she must move into this housing, and out of her hotel room, the day she returned from the hospital after giving birth:

> When I am discharged from the hospital, then I straight went to the housing office and got keys. Then I go to the hotel. And she said, 'You have to leave the hotel.' And also the manager, he said, 'You have to leave the hotel, we don't have … you have to leave today.' So, then I ring my social worker and I asked her, 'Please give me one night, I even can't stand up. How I can pack the things or move?' And she

said, 'Okay, I will check with my manager.' And they gave me one night … They should know after birth you don't have any energy. How can we do things like that? Moving is really hard. We were living there for six months, we have so much stuff.

Maternity care, the 'ideal birthing citizen', and the proliferating matrix of bordering processes

The impact of bordering processes around income and housing extends beyond the reach of these services. The reproductive justice framework highlights the importance of a holistic analysis of the ways in which multiple discursive and policy regimes interact in constraining reproductive autonomy. Applying the framework to the effect of bordering processes illuminates how different iterations of bordering practices and processes, associated with different aspects of social citizenship, interact with each other in complex ways, sometimes reinforcing and sometimes mitigating each other in migrants' lived experiences, and in the creation of stratified reproduction. Bordering processes around income and adequate housing served to limit some of my participants' access to maternity services, thereby overlapping with, and reinforcing, NHS bordering. However, this interaction, and the resulting reproductive stratification, was shaped by the specificities of the NHS as a bordering site, and the practices and philosophies embedded in NHS maternity services. The norm of the 'ideal birthing citizen', in particular, informed how bordering processes around income and housing stratified access to maternity care.

As previously outlined, there is an 'ideal birthing citizen' underpinning *Better Births*, the National Maternity Review for England (2016) – the person who 'should' be reproducing the nation state. This construction is heavily informed by neoliberal discourses around 'responsible reproductive citizenship' that ignore wider structural obstacles to maternal health. The 'ideal birthing citizen' is fully engaged with maternity services, attending appointments, and makes 'good choices' with regard to her health and to her maternity care, both for her own benefit and to improve NHS services (National Maternity Review, 2016). *Better Births* (National Maternity Review, 2016: 84–85), for example, calls on pregnant women to 'engage in a relationship with her own midwife and other health professionals' and '[accept] help to give up smoking, [have] a healthy diet and [be] physically active'. The existence of obstacles to engaging with care or making and enacting choices is dealt with in a cursory manner. Specialist services are recommended for the especially vulnerable, but beyond this, the 'extra support' available to marginalized pregnant women appears to consist mainly of health professionals keeping an open mind and spending more time with patients where necessary, which, in practice, may be difficult to implement given severe understaffing within NHS midwifery services (see Chapter 2). Furthermore, women in need of additional support are grouped under the category 'women from a different background', implying that 'standard' pregnant women are able to engage with health services and make 'good' choices independently. This presumption of autonomy compounded obstacles to accessing maternity care produced by bordering processes around income and housing, as I now explore.

Financial obstacles to accessing maternity care

The poverty produced by bordering processes emerged in interviews as a potential obstacle to accessing maternity care; this echoes Phillimore's (2016) findings regarding the experiences of pregnant migrants in Birmingham (see also Lonergan, 2024a). Helen, a specialist GP in Kirklees, said of one of her asylum-seeking patients: 'We couldn't get her to appointments, you know, she didn't have money, she couldn't access any money. It often comes down to the care is there on the NHS but getting people to it is not thought about.'

This was also echoed by Huda, who works in the third sector supporting migrants and suggested that NHS staff should be educated on how financial barriers might prevent some migrant women from engaging with NHS maternity services: 'Because then they can understand that at some phases of these processes, that these women don't have shelter, they don't have welfare, so they can't go to appointments because of the money, or maybe the taxi.'

Michelle, who is seeking asylum, gave birth during the Covid pandemic, and her baby spent some time in the Neonatal Intensive Care Unit. Worried about catching Covid on the bus, Michelle tried to take taxis to visit her baby in hospital as often as she could, but this was prohibitively expensive on asylum support: 'I have to take taxi every day, everything like that, but sometimes when there is no money anymore to take taxis, I have to leave it maybe two or three days before I go there, but I call, I call the people every day.'

The stratified access to maternity services created by travel costs was further exacerbated for some migrants by their geographic location and changes to maternity services. Recent NHS restructuring has involved consolidating specialist services, including maternity services, in one hospital in a particular trust or area. For some pregnant people, this may mean their nearest services are at some distance. Alison, an obstetrician in West Yorkshire, said in her interview that she felt the consolidation, in general, improved maternity services, but that it could create barriers for impoverished patients:

Gwyneth:	When you say that you think it might mean that people aren't able to access care, in what way?
Alison:	Quite simply they might not be able to get to the hospital. You know, if you've got a baby that's not moving, and

> you've got to trek out of hours all the way to [hospital],
> and you live in [city at the other end of the trust area],
> it's a long way, isn't it?

Farah works in the third sector supporting migrant women, in a location some distance from the nearest maternity hospital. She discussed how, for one of her clients, this distance proved an obstacle to attending antenatal appointments:

Farah: And I know a mum, through the pregnancy, she had …
                I can't remember exactly what was the problem. She has
                to go to hospital every week for a check-up.
Gwyneth: And they couldn't do it in [Town A]?
Farah: No.
Gwyneth: Okay.
Farah: She has to go to [Town B]. And that was really difficult
                for her. And she said, it's so expensive for her.

Dispersal and access to maternity care

As discussed previously, asylum seekers' access to housing comes with the possibility of dispersal – being moved, at little notice, to a new residence, often in a different city. For pregnant migrants, dispersal disrupts access to maternity services and continuity of carer. Pregnant migrants may be separated from the midwifery team caring for them and relocated to a new area where they are likely not even registered with a GP, never mind in contact with maternity services (Feldman, 2013). Given the emphasis in *Better Births* (National Maternity Review, 2016) on the importance of continuity of carer for safer pregnancies and deliveries (see Chapter 2), the policy of dispersing pregnant people highlights both the extent to which the state devalues pregnant migrants' lives as well as their exclusion from the 'ideal birthing citizen' underpinning NHS maternity services. In theory, the government has pledged not to disperse pregnant people after 34 weeks of pregnancy, but in practice, as Marie says, 'there's a failure to adhere to those guidelines'.

Sana was in fact dispersed to a new city 6 days before giving birth and described how difficult this was in her interview:

> It was about six days left in delivery, I didn't had any midwives, I didn't knew any hospitals in [city], so it was just … it was a nightmare, I would say. But I was – I was struggling to get note from people that could guide me where to go.

She also discussed having to give birth without her husband present because he was needed to look after their other two children, as they didn't have any friends in their new city who could help them. She found this very upsetting and stressful:

> And then, obviously my husband was looking after children, and I had to come alone, and when I was in the lift, in the taxi, I was just crying, and I had a little bag on me, and I was thinking 'oh dear, I don't know if I will ever go back'. I thought, I was feeling so disappointed with everything.

While Sana's situation was especially disturbing, dispersing pregnant migrants earlier in their pregnancy may still limit their access to medical care. In her interview, Helen discussed the difficulties facing dispersed pregnant migrants attempting to register with a new GP: 'it's a new place, just finding your way round unless someone is assisting you in that, so we have a problem with people even managing to register unless someone physically helps them with it.'

Farah similarly emphasized the importance she placed on ensuring any newly dispersed pregnant clients were registered with a GP, and the difficulties involved in doing so:

> If they say they are pregnant, I make sure they are seeing the doctor, the midwife. They have been registered. They get all the help from NHS. So sometimes it's not easy, because they are not in one place. So… or maybe they are here for a short time, to this town. [?] … But at least, you know, if they have got the record, you know, make sure they are registered with a doctor. That's important, yeah.

Interacting bordering regimes, stratified reproduction, and the 'deserving' migrant

Bordering processes around income and housing thus also serve to stratify access to NHS maternity services, effectively expanding and reinforcing bordering around NHS maternity care (Lonergan, 2024a). Moreover, this may be compounded by the autonomy expected of the 'ideal birthing citizen'. However, these multiple bordering processes may also interact in ways that serve to mitigate the reproductive injustice and stratification experienced by some pregnant migrants, shaped by different aspects of NHS maternity services as a bordering site. While *Better Births* (National Maternity Review, 2016) may expect a degree of self-sufficiency from the 'ideal birthing citizen', within other discourses, as noted earlier, pregnant migrants are constructed as an especially vulnerable and therefore deserving group. This perceived deservingness, and the impact of bordering processes on access to the resources necessary for a healthy pregnancy, including NHS maternity care, may prompt some midwives to intervene to support their patients in negotiating these processes. As noted previously, these interventions can be read as acts of 'resilience' and 'reworking' (especially where, as discussed later, they involve securing resources for pregnant migrants) (Katz, 2004). They pose an implied challenge not only to discourses devaluing and stigmatizing the reproductive activities of migrant women, but also to the expectation that the 'ideal birthing citizen' demonstrate self-sufficiency in managing her reproductive health.

As previously indicated, some of the healthcare workers I interviewed recognized how bordering processes beyond the NHS charging regime might stratify access to maternity services. Salma, for example, emphasized that pregnant migrants might have 'social risks', that is, risks to their health and pregnancy brought about by the conditions in which they were forced to live, rather than by pre-existing medical conditions. She was committed to bending protocol, where necessary, to address these 'risks':

> So, the social risks might ... Somebody at the Home Office might move somebody around the country. They might miss their scan appointment. Bad outcome health-wise. The social miss ... like, she's got no GP when she turns up here. So, what do you do? Do you say, 'Oh, she needs a GP before she comes here?' No, I don't think so.

This recognition exists at more institutional scales as well. The Royal College of Midwives (2021a), for example, has published a 'pocket guide' titled 'Caring for vulnerable migrant women' that reminds midwives that 'women may need support with basic needs, such as food, clothing and shelter' and makes suggestions on how to mitigate the disruption of care caused by dispersal. Similarly, two of my fieldwork locations had established specialist services for asylum-seeking and other newly arrived 'vulnerable' pregnant migrants.

Additionally, some NHS clinical staff, whether they worked for specialist services or not, would support their patients in negotiating the other forms of reproductive stratification produced by the UK immigration system (Lonergan, 2024a). Ruth, for example, described in her interview supporting recently resettled refugees in bidding for social housing as their existing residence was unsuitable for a baby. Some of my asylum-seeking participants, especially, talked about the additional support they received from their midwife in negotiating the impact of bordering processes. Elior, for example, described her midwife as 'so good', elaborating:

> She was there for me. Any time I call, any time when I call, she picked up, 'Oh, hello darling, how are you?' She come over to my house when

I am pregnant. She went all the way to the charities organisation, bring clothes to my door with her family.

Lisa, who is also an asylum seeker, had a specialist midwife in addition to her 'regular' NHS midwife, and discussed how helpful her specialist midwife was in applying for a maternity grant from the Home Office: 'Yeah, she helped me to write a letter to the migrant help for asking for the maternity grant… She helped me to write down with the details. She gave me the maternity certificate [necessary for the application] before the midwife from the NHS.'

Lisa later spoke about how it was this specialist midwife who also informed her that she was entitled to extra financial support from the Home Office for her baby.

Once again, not all NHS clinical staff were aware of the impact of UK bordering regimes on pregnant migrants, or sympathetic to migrants. Often when asked about challenges facing pregnant migrants, the NHS staff I interviewed would discuss language barriers, but only those involved with specialist services mentioned asylum support or NRPF. Furthermore, as noted earlier, Marie felt that some NHS staff had what she described as 'Daily Mail-y' views about migrants. Jill relayed an anecdote about a woman she supported, whose experience of inadequate housing due to the immigration system was aggravated by racism from a midwife:

> One thing that stuck in my mind was someone who had had a baby very recently and she was complaining to the midwife, when they visited her at home, but she was living in a grotty B&B, and she was saying, 'I'm having to wash the bottles in the sink in the bathroom bit.' And the midwife just said, 'Well, you're from Africa.' You know. 'Surely this is a step up' sort of thing. And she was very upset telling me about this. I couldn't believe.

Furthermore, in Chapter 5, I will discuss at length the multiple ways in which migrant women's exclusion from the model of the 'ideal birthing citizen' results in stratified reproduction and reproductive injustice, including substandard treatment, racism, and obstetric violence on the part of NHS clinical staff. Nonetheless, the interventions of some NHS staff mitigating the impact of bordering processes around financial support and housing indicate the ways in which the multiplication and proliferation of bordering processes may open new opportunities for subversion and resistance.

Conclusion

Bordering processes around social citizenship serve as instruments of reproductive stratification, differentially distributing access to resources needed for a safe and healthy pregnancy according to immigration status. This stratification is further variegated according to a range of other factors, including the social and geographic location of a pregnant migrant, and her individual circumstances and resources. The proliferation of bordering processes has expanded the state's intervention into migrant women's reproductive tasks and the resultant reproductive stratification, as pregnant migrants may now encounter the border at a wide range of sites critical to reproduction. Furthermore, as bordering processes multiply, they may interact with and reinforce each other, hence policies such as NRPF and dispersal not only limit some pregnant migrants' access to adequate income and housing, but also undermine their ability to engage with maternity services. This was expressed by Farah, describing how chaos produced by interacting bordering processes may cause pregnant migrants to deprioritize their own health:

> So, they have got all this worry to think about, so they kind of push themselves at the end of the queue, you know. This pregnancy is not important ... I don't mean they don't care about it, but they have got bigger deals, because – because no money, they have got no money. Money to feed the children, taking children into school. They haven't got shelter.

However, bordering processes are situated, and shaped by the site or service with which they are associated. With regard to maternity services, professional commitments may lead some NHS clinical staff to undermine or mitigate the impact of the NHS bordering regime, even as racialized and gendered discourses that construct pregnant migrants as illicitly using NHS resources may lead others to enforce the border. Moreover, the proliferation and interaction of bordering processes means that practices and philosophies at one site may undermine processes centred around other services. Some NHS clinical staff, especially those associated with specialist services for asylum-seeking pregnant women, may take action to support their patients in negotiating wider bordering processes, including NRPF and dispersal. Importantly, there is a significant degree of arbitrariness here, as this support depends upon the individual views and expertise of NHS staff and the availability of specialist services. The proliferation of bordering processes has thus complicated and variegated the stratification of reproduction, both expanding the scope and severity of state intervention and providing opportunities for resistance and mitigation.

The stratification produced by proliferating bordering processes is compounded by the 'ideal birthing citizen' constructed in *Better Births*, which assumes that pregnant women accessing the NHS face no significant structural obstacles in engaging with maternity services and making 'good choices' about their care. In Chapter 5, I explore the exclusion produced by the 'ideal birthing citizen' in more detail, as well as the reproductive injustice experienced by pregnant and birthing migrants negotiating a maternity system that was not designed for them.

5

The Pregnant Migrant and the 'Person' in 'Personalized Care'

Introduction

> But maybe I would be more confident if I was in my own country either in Poland or, you know, or a British person in the UK, maybe I would make a bigger deal of it. That delay in getting information. Because it wasn't an hour of delay or two hours. I was so desperate that I just sat down on the bed 10 hours after C-section on another bed and I went down to another unit to see what's happening. So, I had to be pretty angry and really stressed to do that.

The quote above is from Agata, an Eastern European migrant who moved to the UK pre-Brexit, describing her experience immediately after giving birth via C-section. Her daughter had been taken to the Neonatal Intensive Care Unit without her knowledge, and she was desperate to find out where her baby was. However, she felt, as an immigrant, that she could not make too much of a fuss, lest she be seen, in her words, as an 'Eastern European girl who is, you know, loud or making problems'. Agata's experience points to the challenges pregnant and birthing migrants may face in negotiating a maternity system that may not reflect their needs, within a wider context in which their reproductive practices may be constructed as threatening to the nation state.

This chapter takes as its starting point the role of maternity services in the reproduction of the nation state; as already noted in Chapter 2, maternity care is not merely about healthcare but 'the reproduction of society' (De Vries et al, 2002b: xii). Maternity care is informed by contestations around how the nation state should be reproduced, and by whom, and the rights and entitlements of birthing people. It both reflects and contributes to discourses around reproductive citizenship and constructions of 'good' reproductive citizens. Throughout this book, I have argued that there is an 'ideal birthing citizen' constructed through NHS maternity policy and practice, the model of who 'should' be reproducing the English nation state and what is expected of them. In this chapter, I explore how my participants' experiences of care were shaped by the extent to which they were able to conform to this norm. Failure to do so, and thereby to demonstrate that one can be trusted to reproduce the nation state correctly, can mean poorer quality maternity care, neglect, or even outright harm and obstetric violence. Discourses around 'responsible reproductive citizenship' thus emerge as an important driver of reproductive injustice in maternity care. Moreover, while my focus is on England, maternity care in other countries will similarly be informed by nationally-specific constructions of who 'should' be reproducing the nation state, and, as I indicate later, across high-income countries, models of the 'ideal birthing citizen' often share key traits.

Women have long been constructed as responsible for the biological and social reproduction of the nation state. However, what this means with regard to pregnancy and childbirth has evolved over the last several decades, shaped by feminist campaigns for greater bodily autonomy in pregnancy and childbirth, debates between advocates of 'natural' and 'medicalized' childbirth, and the emergence of 'healthism', that is, the idea that citizens have a responsibility to safeguard their own health (see Chapter 2) (Crawford, 1980; 2006; Brown and Baker, 2012; McIntosh, 2012; Oakley, 2016). Under neoliberalism, women are expected to engage in 'responsible reproductive citizenship' by, among other things, making 'good choices' with regard to their maternity care. Moreover, in Europe and North America, this maternity care is informed by the interaction of racialized understandings of citizenship and belonging with medical discourses that pathologize the bodies of racially minoritized women, resulting in significant reproductive injustice, including poorer medical care and violations of bodily autonomy (Bridges, 2011; Davis, 2019a; 2019b; Birthrights, 2022; Peter et al, 2022; Sowemimo, 2023).

Additionally, in England, migrants' experiences of maternity care occur within the wider context of a crisis within maternity services, and NHS services more broadly. As noted in Chapter 2, the NHS has been underfunded for the last several years and is consistently missing key performance targets (Anandaciva and Ward, 2019; Ham, 2023; Anandaciva, 2024). Maternity services are both understaffed and underfunded; there is a shortage of roughly 2,000 full-time midwives in England (Royal College of Midwives, 2022a). There have been a series of high-profile scandals and subsequent reviews of maternity services across multiple locations in England (Knight and Bevan, 2021; Royal College of Midwives, 2021b; Knight and Stanford, 2022), with understaffing found to be a significant cause of poor care (Royal College of Midwives, 2021b; Knight and Stanford, 2022).

I begin this chapter with a detailed discussion of the 'ideal birthing citizen' in England underpinning *Better Births*, the National Maternity Review for England (2016). This 'ideal birthing citizen' is an autonomous, self-actualizing individual who behaves responsibly by acquiring and synthesizing information and then acting on this information, in order to make 'good choices' for herself, her family, and, especially, her baby, and indeed, for the improvement of NHS maternity services generally. Drawing on both wider literature and my interviews with migrant mothers and NHS staff, I then consider other characteristics of the 'ideal birthing citizen', locating these within wider discourses around citizenship and reproduction. The 'ideal birthing citizen' – the model for reproducing the nation state 'correctly' – is white, speaks fluent English, is confident negotiating NHS maternity services, and makes 'good' choices. People who do not conform to this model may experience significantly inadequate maternity care, or even obstetric violence.

Better Births and the 'ideal birthing citizen'

Reproductive citizenship and the ethos of sacrifice

The role of maternity services in the reproduction of the nation state is critical to how these services are organized and delivered. As a form of healthcare, maternity care is informed by discourses around citizenship as they pertain to health, and the related rights and responsibilities of citizens (see Chapter 2). As I discuss in more detail later, neoliberal restructuring within the NHS, and the emergence of 'healthism' – the expectation that citizens take responsibility for their own health – has influenced the current provision of maternity care in the UK. However, unlike, for example, renal care, maternity care is also informed by discourses around the reproduction of the nation state: *who* should be reproducing the nation state; *how* the nation state should be reproduced, not just biologically, but also socially and culturally; and the rights and responsibilities of citizenship, as they pertain to reproduction.

Under (neo)liberalism, women's responsibility for reproducing the nation state is understood, on the one hand, as a matter occurring within the private domain of the home, and therefore nothing to do with citizenship. Women should therefore expect neither support from the state nor recognition as citizens for reproductive labour. On the other hand, because of the importance of reproduction to the continuity of the nation state, women's reproductive practices are also seen as a legitimate site for state intervention, and as a pretext for disciplining women's behaviour (Pateman, 1989; Erel, 2011). The paradoxical approach to reproduction in (neo)liberal discourses around citizenship is partly resolved through the construction of women as 'natural' mothers. Women's reproductive activities are not 'political', and therefore nothing to do with citizenship, if they are doing their 'natural' duty (Pateman, 1992).

Central to natural motherhood is an ethos of sacrifice (Lowe, 2016). 'Good' motherhood involves doing what is best for one's children, at the expense of one's own preferences and wellbeing (Lowe, 2016), and 'responsible reproductive citizenship' for women means prioritizing the national reproductive future (see Chapter 1). This ethos of sacrifice has persisted through the emergence of neoliberal discourses of health citizenship that associate greater freedom of choice for patients with greater responsibility to make 'good choices' (Brown and Baker, 2012; Brookes, 2021). For birthing people, this means taking responsibility and making good choices for the health of one's baby (Malacrida and Boulton, 2014; Lowe, 2016; Hooberman et al, 2023). The ethos of sacrifice and the shift towards 'healthism' are compatible with both 'natural' and 'medicalized' models of childbirth.[1] Both models require birthing people to make 'good choices' to prioritize the wellbeing of their baby, and the national reproductive future, whether that means submitting oneself to medical expertise in order to overcome the inherent deficits of the pathologized female body (Fox and Worts, 1999; Lupton, 2012), or undertaking vaginal childbirth without pain relief because this is seen as both morally superior and better for the baby (Beckett, 2005; Lupton, 2012; Hooberman et al, 2023).

The evolving 'ideal birthing citizen' in England

In the 1970s, when childbirth was heavily medicalized in the UK, responsible reproductive citizenship required women to submit themselves to the expertise of doctors, in order to safeguard the health of the baby (Davis, 2012; McIntosh, 2012; Oakley, 2016). McIntosh (2012: 112–113) summarizes the view expounded in the short report (Parliament. House of Commons, 1980) on perinatal and neonatal mortality[2] as '[w]omen's choice would necessarily have to be sacrificed on the altar of safety'. This disregard for women's bodily autonomy was challenged by patients' rights campaigns, natural childbirth activists, and the second-wave feminist movement, all of which emphasized the right of women to make decisions around labouring and birth (Mold, 2010; Davis, 2012; McIntosh, 2012; Oakley, 2016). Concurrently, as noted earlier, the emergence of 'healthism' placed greater emphasis on health as an individual responsibility, while the advent of neoliberalism eroded state support for reproduction, such that responsible reproductive citizenship for women increasingly involved being economically self-sufficient (Lonergan, 2015).

These shifts in the construction of responsible reproductive citizenship are visible in the 'ideal birthing citizen' underpinning *Better Births* (National Maternity Review, 2016). The 'ideal birthing citizen' of *Better Births* is engaged and informed and takes responsibility for her own health and that of her baby. As discussed in Chapter 4, she is self-actualizing and autonomous; in keeping with neoliberal discourses around health citizenship, both barriers to engagement with maternity services and wider social determinants of health are largely disregarded within *Better Births*. The 'ideal birthing citizen' makes 'good choices' about her maternity care, for herself, for her baby, and to safeguard NHS services in general. Information is made available to the 'ideal birthing citizen' to support her in making these choices, but it is she who is ultimately responsible for undertaking research. The role of the health professionals is to *discuss* the information with a pregnant woman and support her in enacting her choices. Summarizing the information-gathering sessions undertaken by the review panel, *Better Births* (National Maternity Review, 2016: 33), for example, states:

> Women and their families told us they need to be able to *access* appropriate information to enable them to make genuinely informed decisions about their care and where to give birth. They wanted information to be evidence-based and *available to them* in a range of formats, including online. They wanted information to be *accessible when they needed it*, to include locally relevant information about the services available, *and for there to be time to discuss the information with a healthcare professional.* (Emphasis added)

The 'ideal birthing citizen' then uses the information she seeks out and discusses with her midwife to make decisions about what kind of care she wants, including where she will give birth, considering not only what is best for herself, but for her family.[3]

In doing so, the 'ideal birthing citizen' improves not only her own birthing experience, and promotes the health of herself and her baby, but also helps to improve NHS maternity services for everyone. *Better Births* (National Maternity Review, 2016: 84) in fact calls on pregnant women (and their families) to be 'powerful agents for change ... by making well-informed choices to ensure safe, personalised care is built around them'. Maternity outcomes will be improved, in this view, not through wider reforms to address the structural determinants of maternal health, but through individual women making 'good' choices (Browne, 2016). With regard to place of birth, in particular, because the 'money follows the mother', patient choice is constructed as a quality control mechanism; pregnant women will make the rational choice to give birth at the 'best' hospitals and birthing centres, financially rewarding those institutions, while poorly-performing hospitals are encouraged to improve (see also Chapter 2).

The 'ideal birthing citizen' of *Better Births* thus reflects not only discourses around 'healthism' (see Chapter 2) and health citizenship, but broader models of 'good' motherhood under neoliberalism. As Lowe (2016) argues, making the 'right' choices around maternity care is part of being a 'good' mother. A woman who is able to take responsibility for her health and that of her baby, stay engaged with NHS services, and make informed choices about pregnancy and childbirth that consider her family's needs, is a woman who will be a good mother and model responsible neoliberal citizenship to the children she raises. She can be trusted to reproduce the nation state 'properly'. Strikingly, *Better Births* (National Maternity Review, 2016: 15) suggests that pregnancy may be the ideal time to inculcate women with the values of good neoliberal motherhood, and shape the raising of future citizens:

> Pregnancy, the birth and the early weeks of a child's life are a crucial period for the future of the family and of the child. For babies, this period has a major influence on their physical, social, emotional and language development. For mothers and the wider family, pregnancy may be the first time they have sustained contact with health services and so presents the ideal opportunity to *influence their lifestyle* and to *maximize their life chances*. (Emphasis added)

In the rest of this chapter, I will draw on the wider literature and the experiences of my participants in considering the traits of the present-day iteration of the 'ideal birthing citizen', produced through the interaction of discourses and practices around citizenship, reproduction, and health. In doing so, I will explore how the 'ideal birthing citizen' creates reproductive injustice and stratification for individuals who are unable to conform to the model.

The 'ideal birthing citizen' is white

Throughout this book, I have discussed racism as a key force structuring UK citizenship and bordering processes, and their relationship with reproduction. Racially minoritized women, regardless of citizenship status, are seen as less capable of reproducing the nation state 'correctly', and their reproductive practices constructed as potentially threatening and legitimate targets of state intervention (Bassel and Emejulu, 2017; Bryan et al, 2018; Coddington, 2020; see also Chapter 1). Given the role of maternity care in the reproduction of the nation state, it is not surprising that this care is shaped by racialized understandings of citizenship; as indicated in Chapter 2, and as I will now discuss more fully, *Better Births* constructs the 'default' consumer of maternity services as a white woman (National Maternity Review, 2016). This is compounded by medical discourses and practices that pathologize the bodies of racially minoritized women.

Medical racism and maternity care

From the 18th century onwards, scientific discourses constructing race as biological, and the bodies of racialized persons as inherently inferior and pathological, were critical to projects of imperialism and enslavement (Hoberman, 2012; Sowemimo, 2023). Medical racism, in combination with gendered discourses around women's reproductive capacities, served to produce racially minoritized, especially black, women as a particularly stigmatized and devalued group subject to significant reproductive injustice (Roberts, 2017). Black people have been constructed within discourses of medical racism as especially 'hardy', a myth that was used to minimize the horrors of the violence enacted on enslaved people (Sowemimo, 2023). The 'hardiness' attributed to black people in general was depicted as allowing black women, endowed with a 'primitive pelvis', to give birth easily and with less difficulty and pain (Bridges, 2011; Hoberman, 2012). In 19th- and early 20th-century Britain, this stereotype of (almost) painless labour was attributed to colonized people in general, as well as to working-class white people,[4] and contrasted with the bourgeois white woman, whose pain in childbirth was indicative of her advanced 'civilization' (Nestel, 1994; Rich, 2016). These stereotypes are sometimes also promulgated by advocates of natural childbirth, with the supposed 'easy labour' of the 'primitive' racialized woman held up as an aspirational model for white women (Nestel, 1994).[5] At the same time, and paradoxically, the higher rates of maternal mortality for black women in the US, the UK, and many other countries where they are subject to racism, has combined with the pathologizing of black women's bodies (Roberts, 2017), and the tendency in medical discourse to treat 'race' rather than 'racism' as a cause of health inequalities, to justify more intensive medical intervention into black women's pregnancies and childbirth (Bridges, 2011; Davis, 2019a; 2019b; Campbell, 2021; Horn, 2023). Racially minoritized birthing women may therefore find themselves both neglected by medical professionals due to their supposed 'hardiness' and also subjected to more intensive medical intervention.

Racism and maternity services in England

There is significant evidence that discourses pathologizing racialized women shape the conceptualization and delivery of maternity care in England. In keeping with the association between Britishness and whiteness in constructions of identity and belonging (see Chapter 1), the birthing woman of *Better Births* (National Maternity Review, 2016) is presumed to be white by default. Race and ethnicity are rarely mentioned in *Better Births*, and specific support for 'families from Black and Minority Ethnic (BME) backgrounds' (36) is discussed under the heading of 'Care for women from different backgrounds' (35), positing a white 'norm' and BME as 'different'. Recent reports into racial injustice in maternity care by the campaigning organizations Birthrights (2022) and FiveXMore (Peter et al, 2022) (which focused specifically on the experience of black women) highlight that the 'white norm' continues to predominate in midwifery training, and that this causes racialized women to receive inadequate care. A case study from the Birthrights (2022: 48) report, for example, quoted a black woman whose baby had severe jaundice that was not recognized by white medical professionals, even after he tested positive:

> At the hospital the doctor admitted the reading was very high but insisted from the look of him there is nothing to suggest he was severely jaundiced, just a 'slight' yellowing of his eyes. By then he looked neon to me .... The white staff did not recognise jaundice in a black baby.

Similarly, the recent report by the All-Party Parliamentary Group on Birth Trauma (2024) included evidence given by a South Asian woman, Neera Ridley-Mayor, detailing how medical professionals had failed to recognize that she has experiencing a major obstetric haemorrhage, because her skin had gone 'ashy' rather than pale. One of my participants, Noor, a midwife working in Greater Manchester, also raised the persistence of the white norm as a problem:

> So, in university we are taught a norm, indirectly. We are taught things that make us expect certain things, and therefore make us, when we are not able to recognise those due to skin colour etc, we are not able to recognise a deteriorating or unwell patient. And this is in numerous ways, for example, the pink baby. Because a [missed] [00:24:54] score says that we need to score a pink baby, but a black baby isn't gonna be pink.

At the same time, the bodies of racially minoritized women may be pathologized and race, rather than racism, treated as a cause of heightened maternal mortality among racially minoritized women. One of the very few mentions of ethnicity in *Better Births* (National Maternity Review, 2016: 56) is as a 'risk factor' that must be taken into account when deciding whether to make a rapid referral to specialist care. Similarly, in an attempt to address the disproportionate maternal mortality of BME women (discussed later), the National Institute for Health and Care Excellence (NICE) proposed that ethnic minority women should have labour induced once their pregnancies had reached 39 weeks, even if there were no other complications (Douglass and Lokugamage, 2021); this was withdrawn after significant resistance (Torjesen, 2021).

There are also significant racialized disparities in the experiences, and outcomes, of maternity care in England. Between 2019 and 2021, black women were almost four times as likely to die in childbirth in the UK as white women, and mixed race and Asian women almost twice as likely (Knight et al, 2023). This data does not include 'near misses' or long-term illness or disability resulting from traumatic births. Additionally, the wider literature indicates that racially minoritized women have worse experiences of maternity care than their white counterparts. Racially minoritized women are subject to stereotyping and racist assumptions on the part of medical professionals (Jomeen and Redshaw, 2013; Garcia et al, 2015; Firdous et al, 2020; Birthrights, 2022; Peter et al, 2022); may not always receive culturally sensitive or appropriate care (Jomeen and Redshaw, 2013; Aquino et al, 2015; Birthrights, 2022; Peter et al, 2022); and report feeling that they were not given the information they needed by healthcare professionals and were not involved in decisions regarding their care (Henderson et al, 2013; Jomeen and Redshaw, 2013; Peter et al, 2022). Echoing research from the US (see Davis, 2019a; 2019b), the FiveXMore (Peter et al, 2022) report also discussed at length the difficulty black women have in accessing pain relief of their choice, stating:

> Although medical reasons may partially explain why over half of Black women reported not receiving their preferred method of pain relief, there is no such reasoning for why an explanation and consultation about the decision that was made, was not provided. There is a historical pattern of medical professionals making decisions on behalf of Black people, lacking the person-centred approach championed by the NHS and eroding personal autonomy and the right to choose – concepts central to the medical profession. Many Black women reported that their pain was not taken seriously and despite requesting support to manage their pain, comments experienced by Black women in this study such as, 'women like you…', 'big and strong', 'you don't look like you need it' evidence racist assumptions and a false belief of greater pain tolerance in Black people. (35)

As discussed in Chapter 1, the migrants I interviewed for this project were from a range of ethnic, racial, and national backgrounds, and some – the white North Americans and Western Europeans – would almost certainly have been perceived as white by medical professionals, and therefore were not impacted by the racist discourses and practices discussed above. However, the majority of my participants were from racially minoritized groups; I include in this description white Central and Eastern European women because of the hostility towards Central and Eastern Europeans in the press and political discourse around Brexit. Indeed, Laura, who is from Central

Europe, discussed feeling like she was being given a dirty look by a nurse when she was speaking to her newborn baby in her first language:

> And when our son was born and they gave him on my chest, I talked to him in [language]. Because I talked to him in [language] the whole pregnancy, you know … So yeah, I was like 'welcome' and something and [my husband] said that one nurse was looking at me like really like, 'Oh my God, what's that she speaks to him?' You know, like… like, it wasn't nice, that was this look like, 'Oh my God,' you know.

Laura had her baby in 2019 and linked this hostility to the Brexit debate, a useful reminder that healthcare professionals may internalize the wider racialized discussions occurring in their societies (Hoberman, 2012).

Relatively few of my migrant participants explicitly framed their negative experiences in terms of racism or racial discrimination. However, there are several caveats that must be acknowledged here: participants may have felt less comfortable naming something as racist to a white Canadian woman; this may have been compounded by the fact that interviews had to be conducted over the phone or via Microsoft Teams because of Covid, thereby making it harder to build rapport between myself and interviewees; participants may have been wary of being seen as complaining 'too much' (and indeed, some explicitly did discuss this with regard to their maternity care, as I elaborate upon later); and, as relative newcomers to the UK, participants' uncertainty regarding what they should expect from NHS maternity care (again, discussed later) may have made it difficult for them to identify specific incidents as related to racism. For example, Humaira, who is Asian, had her request for an epidural denied because she was told she did not 'need' it; she said this made her very angry, but did not frame it as an experience of racism. Anna similarly shared a story from a friend who, like her, is from Eastern Europe, and who was told she wouldn't 'need' painkillers because women from her country are 'hard'. Interestingly, both incidents echo Bridges' (2011) analysis of the way in which staff at a New York hospital constructed birthing women who relied on Medicaid[6] as an unruly and undeserving population by describing them using classic racist tropes normally applied to black women – for example, black 'welfare queens' making illicit use of government resources – regardless of their ethnicity. Here, Asian women (in Humaira's case) and Eastern European women are constructed as 'other' by framing them as 'hardy', a stereotype, as discussed earlier, applied to black women (Bridges, 2011; Hoberman, 2012).

In a fairly shocking incident, Asmani was asked by the doctor who delivered her daughter by C-section if she was crying out of disappointment:

Asmani: I still remember when my daughter's C-section, the doctor took her out and she was crying and I was start

	crying and the doctor said, 'Are you crying because you have a daughter?' I said no! [laughs]
Gwyneth:	Really?!
Asmani:	Just emotion.
Gwyneth:	So he thought you were sad that you had a girl and not a boy?
Asmani:	Yeah. I think he's just a bit of a mindset for them as well, because they think like Asian people just want a boy.

Some of the NHS staff I interviewed, especially those that were racially minoritized themselves, or worked very closely with racially minoritized patients, also raised the existence of racism within maternity services. Julia is a white British woman and a specialist GP who works with asylum seekers. In her interview, she discussed feeling that her patients received inferior care, but that the discrimination was subtle, making it difficult to directly challenge:

> And I think harder than that really is the feeling that there is discrimination and racism within the NHS which breaks my heart really, you know, that people are looked upon differently. I often think that if I was ringing up and saying Mrs Jane Smith from [affluent neighbourhood in a city] had a problem we'd get a different response from me ringing up with a – for want of a better description a foreign sounding name, although how you define a foreign sounding name is a whole other question. So, it's – that's hard cause you don't often get that very overt comment that you can say no, stop, I'm gonna challenge you there, that's – that's a racist comment or that's a discriminatory comment. It's – it's those subtleties and nuances and people who are just waiting a little bit longer for care or whose care is just a little bit lower standard than – than you might expect.

Joanne, a midwife who is racially minoritized, related the racism she had witnessed to wider structural racism in the UK, pointing to how discourses around citizenship and belonging are reflected in maternity services:

> [T]he prejudices that are there, you can't hide away from them, because these disparities can't continue to exist. You can't just say they have a different anatomy or they're more predisposed to X, Y, Z, you know? But I think it's inherent within the society that we're living in so unless it's done at a national level you will fall straight down. It needs to be addressed within schools.

The 'ideal birthing citizen' speaks English

Over the last few decades, English language fluency has become critical to the construction of racialized discourses around citizenship and racialized bordering processes in the UK (Bassel and Khan, 2021; Fortier, 2021; Khan, 2022). Fortier (2021) argues that language fluency is used to determine the 'integratability' of migrants, and thus contributes to the construction of criteria around entry and settlement (117); moreover, migrants who do not speak fluent English become racialized as 'not (quite) white' (120). The deployment of language in bordering processes has been informed by anxieties around reproduction. Migrant women who do not speak fluent English are constructed as incapable of reproducing the next generation of British citizens, and as posing an obstacle to their children's integration (Yuval-Davis et al, 2005; Lonergan, 2015; Bassel and Khan, 2021).

In keeping with these raciolinguistic discourses around British citizenship, the 'ideal birthing citizen' of *Better Births*, the person who 'should' be reproducing the nation state, is presumed to be fluent in English. There is little mention of language barriers in *Better Births*, beyond noting that for some patients from BME families, personalized care 'might mean taking the extra time to gauge understanding of the language being used at an appointment' (National Maternity Review, 2016: 36), clearly conflating 'Minority Ethnic' and 'immigrant', congruent with racialized discourses around British citizenship. Additionally, it is suggested that where patients have 'difficulty communicating', personalized care might mean 'providing an interpreter or translating the key points into their native language' (36).

As I demonstrate later, providing a patient with the 'key points' is not the same as discussing their care in full and can lead to significant misunderstandings. It also contradicts the emphasis in *Better Births* on the importance of women being engaged with their care and making informed choices. The assumption of English fluency, and how this is implemented, should be additionally read within the context of the funding crisis within the NHS. Telephone interpreters tend to be used for midwifery and hospital appointments rather than in-person interpreters, and these can be difficult and time-consuming to use. The latter may be particularly relevant given the time pressure on midwives. Ruth, a midwife in Leeds, elaborated:

> But also, telephone interpreting is fine as long as you've got a good interpreter on the end. Not somebody doing the washing up or doing another job at the same time. You've got a good connection. And you've not had to wait 20 minutes just to get through to an interpreter. And that, you can't say to your manager ... well you can say it took 20 minutes to get through to an interpreter, therefore my day has been extended [she has been forced to work longer – GL].

The construction of the 'ideal birthing citizen' as fluent in English produces significant reproductive stratification and injustice. Language barriers may prevent women and other birthing people from being able to engage with NHS services and make informed decisions about their care, including giving informed consent. Several of my participants encountered language barriers when trying to engage with maternity services and make decisions around care. Rana and Ines are both Arabic-speaking women who reported being given information sheets in English by their midwives, despite not being able to read English. Rana relied on her husband to translate them for her, while Ines used Google Translate on her phone; this highlights both the resourcefulness of migrant women when dealing with exclusions within NHS maternity services and the extra effort they must go to to engage with these services. Helen, a specialist GP who works with asylum seekers and refugees, discussed the difficulties of finding suitable materials for patients who don't speak English:

> I mean around Covid we've seen masses of increase in translated materials for different languages. But whether that filters down to all issues that need information in other languages is another matter, so it's a bit of a hunt for if you want to send somebody something, you know, unfortunately we do often have to send them it in English and hope that it's written fairly simply.

The availability of information in multiple languages around Covid indicates both a recognition of the importance of such resources and a willingness to spend the money necessary to provide them when it is a question of a public health crisis that also impacts UK citizens.[7]

Furthermore, most of the women I interviewed with the support of an interpreter stated that a professional interpreter was not used in their antenatal appointments, or sometimes even when giving birth. Some reported their midwife using simplified language to discuss their care, allowing them to 'get by'. Zahra, who speaks Arabic, discussed her midwife using simple language in her explanations rather than relying on an interpreter: '[Interpreter]: [The midwife] used to repeat the same things and from repeating the same questions, Zahra understand the thing she is saying like taking the blood, checking her tummy and things like that.'

Given the potential complexity of pregnancy, there is clearly significant possibility in such an arrangement for critical misunderstandings. Other women reported their husband or friends serving as interpreters, which is not ideal. The Royal College of Midwives (2021a) advises against using family members as interpreters. Family and friends may be fluent in English but still struggle to interpret technical medical terms. Furthermore, while many participants made it clear their husband was, in fact, their preferred interpreter,[8] this can also facilitate further abuse in situations of domestic violence and coercive control, especially for migrant women whose immigration status and lack of English language fluency may increase their dependency upon their husband.

In extreme circumstances, the presumption of English language fluency can cause significant reproductive injustice. Women who do not speak or understand English are 25 times more likely to die in pregnancy, childbirth, or postnatally (Rowntree, 2024). Huda, who works in the third sector supporting pregnant migrants, stressed the significance of language barriers during her interview: 'Well language is a barrier because you need to understand why you are going to these appointments, and what's happening, and what you need to do, what is asked from you. And most —some women went into labour not knowing that they were in labour.'

Similarly, in explaining why she felt interpretation was critically important, Joanne related a disturbing anecdote:

> It was a family that they'd transferred over from a different hospital, baby wasn't compatible with life and they'd had some treatment at a tertiary unit to basically stop the baby's heart from beating and start the process of delivering this baby, but they hadn't realised that, because when I walked into the room it was very cheerful and I thought, okay, and so when we spoke about there's going to be no paediatricians, we are not resuscitating the baby and it was kind of like oh my gosh, what? And for that experience, that has actually stayed with me for a long time.

The 'ideal birthing citizen' understands, and can negotiate, NHS maternity services

As previously outlined, the 'ideal birthing citizen' is constructed as autonomous and self-sufficient, and able to be fully engaged with maternity services, in keeping with wider neoliberal discourses around citizenship and health. The role of the wider material and discursive context in constraining reproductive autonomy, highlighted by the reproductive justice framework, is ignored. Wider obstacles to engagement go largely unacknowledged in *Better Births* (National Maternity Review, 2016). Additionally, as discussed in Chapter 2, the 'ideal birthing citizen' is also presumed to be a UK citizen – there is little discussion of the specific challenges facing pregnant and birthing migrants – and therefore to have 'grown up' with the NHS. The difficulties some migrants may experience in navigating a new system is therefore largely unaddressed both within *Better Births* and often (but not always) in practice. Shim's (2010: 3) concept of 'cultural health capital', which she defines as a 'specialized form of cultural capital that can be leveraged in health care contexts to effectively engage with medical providers', provides a useful lens here. Cultural health capital includes, among other things, 'knowledge of medical topics and vocabulary' and the ability to communicate effectively with health professionals (Shim, 2010: 3). It is stratified according to class, race, and other social inequalities, and tends to reproduce these inequalities in the provision and experience of healthcare (Shim, 2010). Although not discussed by Shim (2010), I would argue that cultural health capital should expand to include knowledge of the organization and provision of medical care within a society, and knowledge of the norms and practices around health and 'good' healthcare. An understanding of these norms and practices can be critical to making 'informed choices' around maternity care. In her analysis of the relationship between knowledge, class, and choice in childbirth in the US, Lazarus (1994: 26) argues that 'birth knowledge' includes 'social knowledge', by which she means 'knowledge of medical procedures that occur during pregnancy and birth in addition to institutional knowledge of the hospital as a bureaucracy-who is responsible for what decisions and how a patient can exert pressure to obtain the kind of care she wants'.

Migrants may not possess this knowledge, as they are new to the UK and the NHS, and the expectation that the 'ideal birthing citizen' be autonomous and engaged may be experienced as a lack of support from clinical staff in navigating maternity services.

Some of my participants specifically raised the challenges of negotiating an unfamiliar health system, and the lack of support they felt was forthcoming from clinical staff in helping them address this. Strikingly, many of these women were well-educated and fluent in English. This means they may not have been perceived as 'vulnerable' and therefore in need of extra support by the medical professionals caring for them (see Chapter 4). Additionally, as well-educated, relatively affluent women, they may have had comparatively high levels of cultural health capital in their countries of origin. As such, they may have felt more compelled to behave as 'good' medical consumers and been frustrated by the obstacles created by having to navigate a new system. In the first focus group, Emily noted the difficulties she experienced, and how this impacted her ability to engage with NHS maternity services and make informed choices about care:

> I think for me, I guess some of it is not knowing exactly how to navigate the health system when giving birth. And I sort of, it's not like you know anyway, so if it's your first time giving birth, it's like, you don't know what to expect. But I think there were something things where it wasn't totally clear to me where I could push for, like, you know, I really wanted a midwife-led birth, for example, and I ended up on a consultant ward. And I didn't know how much I could sort of push back and be like, I really want a midwife-led birth instead.

The other participants, Laura and Asra, both agreed, with Laura saying:

> Yeah, that's … you actually said the correct point. The thing is we know how it works in our home countries, right? So, we kind of know from friends and family, and how it's supposed to be. And because we are somewhere else, it's completely different than you thought it will be.

Some less privileged participants also raised it as a challenge. Amal explained through the interpreter (speaking of Amal in the third person here) that her second pregnancy in the UK was easier because she was now experienced with the NHS: 'she used the first experience to know where to go and what questions she expects people to ask her, and she knows the system and she used to go the hospital just on her own because she knew everything.'

Huda discussed how these challenges might be exacerbated for migrants by other inequalities, such as access to technology:

> The system is very different from our countries. And I guess, when you get pregnant, they expect you to know the system. Because you are born in it. But we are not born in this system, so it's very, very new to us. And it's different. And especially now when they have moved things onto digital, and you don't even have your pregnancy file or book and stuff, so it's even harder for these women, if they don't have internet connection, their phones are not that smart. And it's just, you know, getting harder, rather than getting easier, isn't it?

Different expectations regarding care

Furthermore, some of the women I interviewed discussed feelings of disorientation and distress that arose where their expectations regarding 'good maternity care' diverged from NHS standards and practices, and clinical staff did not necessarily take the time to discuss these differences and reassure them. What constitutes 'good maternity care' is contested, and different countries have different standards with regard to medical intervention, frequency of scans and antenatal check-ups, and so on (see De Vries et al, 2002a: for the variation within wealthy Western countries). Many of the women I interviewed were from countries with a more medicalized standard of maternity care. Some of these women made it clear they preferred the NHS model to their country of origin's. Leila, a refugee from the Middle East, very much liked that pregnancy was treated as a 'normal' experience by the NHS:

> I love the way they act with women who are pregnant. They act like it's normal. You can do everything. It's a normal thing. Not you have to be worried a lot. Because in our country, we don't have that culture. In our culture, if anyone was pregnant, you have to rest all the time.

You don't have to do anything, because they're afraid about it. But in this country, I love that way that they acted.

Other women, however, preferred the more medicalized approach of their country of origin. Amara had a difficult first trimester with frequent dizziness; in a previous pregnancy in her country of origin, this had been treated with injections and vitamins, and she was upset she was not given these in the UK:

If I come to compare between the care here and the care back home, I would say the care back home was much better than the care here. If I come back and give you an example about when I faint and they don't even do anything, back home, as soon as I faint, they always give me that injection for energy, or like vitamins.

Habiba had originally come to the UK to rejoin her husband, who is a refugee. Unlike many of my other participants, she was from a country where medical care in pregnancy and childbirth is very poor. She stated in her interview that she had originally planned to give birth vaginally because 'I was afraid of C-section because back home it is very difficult, and it is scary back home'. She was therefore very frightened when she was told during labour that she needed an emergency C-section:

Habiba: So, when the doctor told me that, I was very, very afraid because I have never heard of people who have C-section here and I was a lot scared, very scared. I did not expect it as well, it was scary.

Gwyneth: It must have been very scary.

Habiba: Yes, also I started getting afraid for the baby when they told me the baby is not in the right way. And I got scared for the baby and when they asked me to sign, I simply signed.

Importantly, all of these issues possibly could have been resolved with better communication with medical professionals explaining the reason behind the treatment decisions, or in Habiba's case, ensuring she was well-informed beforehand regarding the quality of maternity care in the UK. Ruth, a midwife in West Yorkshire, raised this issue herself in her interview, and stressed the importance of communication:

So quite a few women are used to having, may have lots of scans, because they're paying for their care. So, the rationale behind what they're doing might not be explained. Whereas we try to give them choices and explain quite clearly using interpreters what their choices are. And hopefully help them to understand the rationale behind the care that they are receiving. Particularly when it varies, sometimes quite significantly, from what they've had at home.

The 'ideal birthing citizen' makes 'good choices' – or may have them made for her

Disregard for bodily autonomy and preferences

As discussed earlier, the 'ideal birthing citizen' is expected to make 'good choices', for herself, for her baby, for her family, and to improve NHS maternity services. Neoliberal discourses around health citizenship, as previously noted, associate the right to make choices around one's care with the responsibility to manage one's health and make 'good choices' (Brown and Baker, 2012; Brookes, 2021). The responsibility to make 'good choices' may be especially fraught regarding maternity care, given its role in the reproduction of the nation state; in choosing well, birthing women are not only demonstrating that they can take responsibility for their own health, but that they can be trusted to reproduce, biologically *and* socially, the next generation of citizens. In this section, I explore some of my participants' experiences of disrespectful treatment during childbirth through the lens of the 'ideal birthing citizen' and anxieties about the reproduction of the nation state.

The World Health Organization (2015) defines 'disrespectful and abusive treatment during pregnancy and childbirth' as encompassing:

> Outright physical abuse, profound humiliation and verbal abuse, coercive or unconsented medical procedures (including sterilization), lack of confidentiality, failure to get fully informed consent, refusal to give pain medication, gross violations of privacy, refusal of admission to health facilities, neglecting women during childbirth to suffer life-threatening, avoidable complications, and detention of women and their newborns in facilities after childbirth due to an inability to pay.

Abusive and disrespectful treatment during birth is generally regarded as a subsection of violence against women, and is sometimes termed 'obstetric violence' (Pickles, 2019; Chadwick, 2021). I agree strongly with van der Waal et al (2023: 93) that obstetric violence must be 'understood as institutionalized intersectional violence', with obstetric racism understood as a separate phenomenon that is nonetheless 'linked to … and productive of' obstetric violence. In particular, I wish to consider abusive and disrespectful treatment during birth through the lens of gendered and racialized discourses around responsible reproductive citizenship, and the expectation that women make 'good' choices' regarding maternity care. There are multiple causes of abusive and disrespectful treatment during pregnancy and childbirth, but I contend that we can usefully read obstetric violence through the lens of anxieties that women are failing to reproduce the nation state 'correctly', and that medical professionals must therefore override their wishes in the national interest. Racialized and migrant women are especially likely to have their wishes disregarded in this context because their ability to reproduce the nation state is already called into question.

There were multiple instances described in my interviews with migrant mothers in which their bodily autonomy and wishes regarding care had clearly been disregarded by medical professionals. As already noted earlier, for example, Humaira was told she did not 'need' an epidural, despite her request. Two of my participants discussed at length having their preference for a C-section disregarded. Hadia was initially told by her midwife that elective C-sections were not performed in the UK, but she did her own research and discovered this was not true. However, her midwife then postponed putting her in touch with the two obstetricians whose permission she required until it was too late:

Gwyneth: So, you were – you were told by the midwife you couldn't have an elective C-section.

Hadia: At the beginning, I wasn't – I was told that I shouldn't even think about it, it's no way. This doesn't happen in the UK, that's what she kept telling me.

              …

Hadia: But then I googled it, and I go – I went on the websites and stuff, and it all says that you have the right to choose, you know …

Gwyneth: Yeah.

Hadia: … the birth plan, the one you like. But then it's not really true, that's not true at all. I – I'm a fighter. I have to – I stood it in every single appointment, that I'm not gonna have normal birth. I'll have a C-section. And then they kept saying OK, we'll get you two doctors who can, you know, like a jury who will talk about it, and you have to convince them, and things, or like – yeah. [laughs] Yeah. And then it didn't happen really.

Hadia ended up having a traumatic birth, which she felt would have been avoided if her request for a C-section had been respected.

Agata had her first baby delivered by emergency C-section, and when she became pregnant again, her midwife referred her to an obstetrician to discuss having another C-section; however, this obstetrician refused because he believed it might prevent her having more children, and ignored her insistence that she did not want more than two:

> [He said] 'Right, okay, I don't really think that you should have a C-section. Because if you have a second C-section, if you want to have a third baby, the risk increases a lot, you can start losing too much blood with the third procedure.' And I said, 'I'm not sure about the third baby, I'm happy with two.' He was like, 'Have a think when you want to complete your family.' But he was quite confident about saying to me, 'No, I'm going to decline your request.'

She was eventually able to be referred to another obstetrician, who agreed to perform the C-section.

Another of my participants, Gabriella, who gave birth at home, reported being repeatedly pressured by her midwife into having a vaginal exam before entering her birthing pool, and she eventually agreed out of exhaustion:

> So then when she came, and she was doing my blood pressure and everything, she was like, 'Oh, I need to check you when I came, and I need to check you before you can go to the pool.' So, I was like, 'Oh, I wasn't really sure if I want vaginal examinations.' And she's like, 'Oh no, but I need to check you before you can get in the pool.' And I remember my husband being like, 'Gabriella, if you don't want it ...' Because I was like, 'Okay, okay, I guess if you need to do it, just do it.' And I remember my husband being like, 'Gabriella, you told me you're not sure if you want it. You told me you don't want it. So, if you don't want it just say, you can decline, like just say no.' But I was like, 'Oh no, it's okay, if she's asking so much for it. If it's such a big deal, let's just do it.' So, it wasn't like the most comfortable. But yeah, that just didn't feel very nice, that she just ignored me a little bit. I said I don't want it, but she kept asking.

Teresa, who is from Southeast Asia, also reported being subjected to a vaginal exam during labour without consent, a clear instance of obstetric violence.

Strikingly, in many of the examples mentioned, women were subject to disrespectful treatment when they were acting as 'informed, engaged choosers', but had come to different conclusions regarding treatment than the medical professionals overseeing their care. Hadia and Gabriella both engaged in significant independent research to establish their rights in childbirth and which treatment options they preferred. In her interview, Irené, a white woman from Western Europe, discussed wanting to have what she considered to be a 'good birth'. This led her to plan a home birth and to refuse induction after her pregnancy passed 42 weeks, opting instead to take things 'day by day'. This involved visiting her local hospital every 2 days for tests to determine whether the baby was in distress. She recalled being warned by the consultant that she was endangering her baby:

> So, I would arrive, and I would have all my test, and a midwife would be, you know, sort of nice, and be, 'Ah, how you feel? Oh, it's all good, oh cool, oh brilliant.' You know, all nice, and then a very stressed person, that is a consultant, rushing, sweating, from meeting to meeting, from jumping from one room to the other, would come, would not ask me – not ask me anything, just be looking at me and say, 'You are overdue… My responsibility is to tell you that what you're doing is wrong. You are endangering yourself, your baby, and here it is.'

She found this upsetting and frustrating, in part because she had done extensive research – in many ways, behaving as the 'ideal birthing citizen' of *Better Births* – and felt that she was being ignored by hospital staff:

> But they were like – they were like, 'Do you realise you're gonna kill your baby,' or, 'You realise that you're really endangering your baby' – you know.
>
> …
>
> … and I can understand that because I know they in the information that they based their opinions, and, you know, when – you know, I had read all the peer-reviewed papers, and the studies, and the statistics about, you know, why, you know, why is that notion of like, you know – I really researched, and I learn, and I look at it myself from the – on why it is considered that after 42 weeks, you know, the baby is in danger. And I, you know, I concluded that those studies were partial, and not fully, you know, outdated, et cetera, et cetera.
>
> …
>
> So – but it was very obvious that they were really not listening to me.

These experiences are not unique to migrants; the recent report from the All-Party Parliamentary Group on Birth Trauma (2024: 8) highlights lack of informed consent as a key issue emerging from their evidence gathering, and also notes that 'women frequently felt they were subjected to interventions they had not consented to'. Similarly, a 2018 report by Birthrights found that only 26 per cent of the trusts they surveyed offered maternal request caesareans 'if appropriate support has been offered and a woman is making an informed decision' (9), while 47 per cent put additional conditions on a maternal request caesarean section and 15 per cent did not offer them at all. Pickles (2019) characterizes this as 'obstetric violence by omission', which she defines as occurring when 'healthcare providers … employ evidence-based guidelines to deny women access to non-clinically indicated care, knowing that this denial of care will cause an infringement of women's psychological integrity'.

However, as discussed repeatedly throughout this book, the reproductive practices of migrant women are a significant source of anxiety, and it is possible that pregnant migrants may be more likely to be seen by medical professionals as making 'bad choices' as a result. Further research comparing the experiences of migrant women and citizens with regard to informed consent and obstetric violence is necessary. Pregnant migrants may also belong to other groups who are more likely to have their wishes disregarded, notably racially minoritized women, and language barriers, and a lack of action taken to address these barriers, will also make it more difficult for some pregnant migrants to communicate their preferences to medical professionals.

At the same time, it is important to recognize many of my participants also reported positive experiences around childbirth and did feel that their wishes were respected. Even where they had a medical intervention they did not want, many accepted their clinician's view that this intervention had been necessary, and did not feel that their autonomy or wishes had been disregarded. Furthermore, discourses of responsible reproductive citizenship are materialized into practices by individual NHS staff and filtered through their individual perceptions and commitments. Alison, an obstetrician in West Yorkshire, firmly stated in her interview that decisions around care would ultimately be up to the patient, even where she disagreed:

> You know, ideally to me [personalized care] means that you see the same person and that you make a plan that they're comfortable with. That's what personalised care means, it means making a plan with them. And I do try and do that with my patients. Often people just tend to follow advice that you give them, but if they don't want to, I try to be supportive of what they want. You know, for example, if I've said, 'I think you should be induced,' and they've said, 'No, I don't want to be,' then I'm like, 'Well that's okay, you know. These are the risks, and these are the things we can do instead, if you don't want to do that.'

Being a respectful guest

Additionally, a few of the women I interviewed discussed not wanting to advocate for themselves too vociferously for fear of being seen as a 'bad guest'. These concerns must be read within the wider context of the proliferation of discourses constructing pregnant migrants as undesirable and threatening, and as coming to the UK to use the NHS and other public services illicitly (see Chapter 2). When asked how being a migrant impacted on her experience of maternity care, Hadia stated that she didn't know what she could ask for and had wanted to be polite as a 'guest' in the UK:

Gwyneth:	Generally speaking, do you feel that being an immigrant made any difference to your experience of pregnancy and childbirth?
Hadia:	I think it made a difference because I didn't really know what I could ask for.
Gwyneth:	OK.
Hadia:	Or was allowed, and… that, yeah, I think it's always different if you're in your own country, you can say no, I just want this. I don't care what others say. But you try to be more polite if you're in different country, and you don't want to be rude, it's like…
Gwyneth:	Why – why do you think that is?
Hadia:	It's like feeling like you're a guest, and you can't really behave badly in somebody's house.

Agata, as noted earlier, was aware of not wishing to be seen as a 'loud Eastern European girl'. In her interview, Laura revealed that she had occasionally returned to her country of origin while pregnant to get additional checks, but was also wary of being seen as 'too critical' of the NHS: 'I just don't want, you know, like, people can say, "Yeah, she's living in England and she is just saying that it's not perfect," or … you know.'

As discussed previously, Laura felt that the Brexit debate and its aftermath had encouraged xenophobia against Central and Eastern European migrants, which likely influenced her perception of what she was 'allowed' to say about the NHS.

The 'ideal birthing citizen' beyond England

While this book focuses on England, maternity policy and practice in other countries will similarly be underpinned by a model of an 'ideal birthing citizen', shaped by nationally-specific hierarchical and multi-tiered discourses around citizenship and who 'should' be reproducing the nation state. These discourses may be materialized in differing policies and practices around maternity care, and in different patterns of reproductive injustice and stratification. Obstetric racism is a feature of maternity services across the Global North, as are disproportionately high rates of maternal mortality and morbidity among racially minoritized and migrant women (Zwart et al, 2011; Ray et al, 2018; Davis, 2019b; Knight et al, 2019; Montalmant and Ettinger, 2024; Arcilla et al, 2025). There are also, however, important national differences in how obstetric racism is constructed, and its influence on policy and practice, further inflected by variations in norms around what constitutes 'good' maternity care. Much of the existing scholarship on obstetric racism is based in the US, and while this scholarship can be fruitfully applied to England, it is grounded in specific histories of violent racialization, as well as a wider context of a heavily medicalized, for-profit healthcare system, which is seen as contributing to the resultant reproductive injustice (Bridges, 2011; Davis, 2019a). By contrast, obstetric racism in England occurs within a socialized, midwifery-led system, albeit one where black women may still be targeted for medical intervention; yet, in both the US and England, black women are 3–4 times more likely to die in childbirth than their white counterparts (Knight et al, 2019; Montalment and Ettinger, 2014). Further granular research is required to better tease out the commonalities and differences in black women's experiences in these two countries.

Similarly, as indicated by the experience of some of my participants, there are significant national variations in norms around medical intervention in pregnancy and childbirth (see also De Vries et al, 2002a). Importantly, both medical and natural models of childbirth are compatible with discourses around responsible reproductive citizenship that require women to make 'good choices' and prioritize their baby, and the national reproductive future, over their own preferences. However, while this ethos of sacrifice may remain consistent across countries, how this is actually experienced by pregnant migrants will vary according to norms around medicalization and the social location and preferences of the patient. Bridges (2011) notes that pregnant people in receipt of Medicaid in the US, including low-income migrants, are constructed as 'unruly' (mentioned earlier) and consequently subject to a high degree of medical intervention in their antenatal care, regardless of their wishes. By contrast, Shan et al (2023) discuss the disparities between the relatively low degree of medicalization of antenatal care in the Netherlands and middle-class Chinese migrants' desire for increased intervention, which 'may result in women experiencing their concerns and anxieties being silenced' (5).

Interestingly, though, many of the key traits of the English 'ideal birthing citizen' appear to be common across the Global North. The wider literature, for example, suggests that in high-income countries, language barriers, and difficulties navigating unfamiliar healthcare systems are common barriers for migrants attempting to access maternity care (Small et al, 2014; Aquino et al, 2015; Phillimore, 2015; 2016; Fair et al, 2020; Obionu et al, 2023; Sudhinaraset et al, 2023). This points to shared features of responsible reproductive citizenship across these countries, including raciolinguistic constructions of belonging, as well as neoliberal discourses around 'healthism' and the expectation that birthing people possess an understanding of local maternity services.

Conclusion

This chapter has looked at the provision of maternity services through the lens of citizenship, arguing that there is an ideal 'person' underpinning 'personalized care' – the person who can be trusted to reproduce the nation state correctly. This 'ideal birthing citizen' is a responsible consumer of maternity services, who seeks out and synthesizes information in order to make 'good choices' for herself, her baby, and her family. In keeping with racialized and raciolinguistic constructions of national belonging, this 'ideal birthing citizen' is also white and fluent in English. As a self-actualizing, autonomous neoliberal citizen, she is able to navigate NHS maternity services, including when faced with standards of treatment that differ from those in her country of origin. Finally, she is able to meet the responsibility of making 'good choices' about her care as understood by medical professionals, and if she fails to do so, she may find her choices overruled. Pregnant migrants unable to meet this norm may be subject to substandard maternity care; have difficulty accessing the information needed to make decisions about their care and communicating these decisions to clinical staff; and, in some cases, even find themselves subject to abusive or disrespectful treatment, with their preferences around care ignored.

In the next and final chapter, I review the findings of this book and what my participants' experiences reveal about the relationship between citizenship, reproduction, and proliferating bordering processes. I apply the lens of reproductive justice to the issue of 'choice' in maternity care, as well as in analyzing the construction of precarious pregnant migrants as an especially abject population, and make some suggestions for implementing the findings of this book to improve migrants' experiences of maternity care.

6

Conclusion: Reproductive Justice for Pregnant and Birthing Migrants

> For the calendar year of 2013, births in the UK to non-UK born mothers accounted for 25% of all live births. That is why we need to reduce immigration. (HL Deb, 16 March 2015)

> At another [citizenship] ceremony, the presiding registrar congratulated new citizens on taking 'a step that will have lasting repercussions on your lives and of course very much on the lives of your children and their children and on generations of your families in the years to come. (Fortier, 2021: 170)

The two quotes above illustrate different aspects of the relationship between reproduction, citizenship, and bordering. The first is from Lord Bates, a Conservative member of the House of Lords, and then a Minister of State at the Home Office, arguing that the hyper-fertility of migrant women necessitated a reduction in immigration. There is a clear implication that the children of the non-UK born mothers are not 'properly' British. The second is from Anne-Marie Fortier's book *Uncertain Citizenship: Life in the Waiting Room*, in which she describes the words of the registrar at a citizenship ceremony, reminding the new UK citizens that their children and grandchildren will now also be British. These new citizens were immigrants the day before, but having successfully met all the criteria for becoming British citizens, they have demonstrated that they can be trusted to reproduce the nation state correctly. Indeed, it may now arguably be their duty to ensure the longevity of the nation state by having children and grandchildren (Fortier, 2021).

Citizenship and reproduction are fundamentally intertwined and mutually constitutive. Reproductive citizenship should be understood as encompassing the rights related to 'with whom may one reproduce and under what social and legal conditions' (Turner, 2008: 53), as well as the ways in which discourses and practices around reproduction mediate citizenship and produce individuals into different locations with regard to hierarchical and multi-tiered constructions of citizenship and belonging. Women's experience of reproductive citizenship is not merely about their rights to access contraception or state-funded childcare; the construction of women as responsible for reproduction is formative of their location within discourses of citizenship and their relationship to the state and their fellow citizens. The reproductive capacities of racially minoritized women, for example, are critical to their construction as potentially threatening to the nation state. Bordering processes reflect and reinforce the mutually constitutive relationship between reproduction and citizenship. The perceived ability to reproduce the nation state 'correctly' contributes to the construction of different individuals and groups as potentially un/desirable migrants and future citizens, and shapes their entitlements and what is expected of them.

At present, the relationship between citizenship and reproduction is being reconfigured, and taking on new salience, due to the convergence of multiple phenomena. The entitlements and responsibilities of citizenship as they relate to reproduction have shifted as a consequence of neoliberal restructuring. Discourses around citizenship under neoliberalism emphasize personal responsibility and economic productivity, while state support for reproduction has become increasingly eroded and conditional. Women are now expected to demonstrate 'responsible reproductive citizenship' by filling the gaps left by the retrenched welfare state; undertaking paid work to demonstrate financial self-sufficiency; raising their children to be autonomous and economically productive citizens; and making 'good choices' with regard to motherhood, including in pregnancy and childbirth. Additionally, while immigration policies have long been informed by, and served to discipline, migrants' reproductive practices, the proliferation and intensification of bordering processes is strengthening the reach of the state in policing these practices. New forms of reproductive injustice and stratified reproduction are emerging as a consequence. Nonetheless, as bordering processes expand to multiple sites, they encounter, and may be shaped, mediated, or even undermined by, the practices and philosophies associated with these sites, and new possibilities for resistance may emerge. Finally, we are also seeing the resurgence of a far right in which 'reproductive racism' is central to both discourse and practice (Erel, 2018; Siddiqui, 2021).

The mutually constitutive relationship between reproduction and citizenship is visible in women's experience of healthcare as a right of social citizenship. The provision and organization of maternity care is not merely an aspect of healthcare as an entitlement of citizenship, but reflects discourses around who should be reproducing the nation state, what is expected of them, and what they are owed. *Better Births*, the National Maternity Review for England (2016), constructs an 'ideal birthing citizen', the model of the person who 'should' be reproducing the nation state. The 'ideal birthing citizen' demonstrates 'responsible reproductive citizenship', consistent with gendered neoliberal discourses that call on women to raise their children with minimal support from the state and model economically productive behaviour to their children. She is engaged with maternity services and able to take responsibility for her own health and, more importantly, her baby's health. She is also self-actualizing and autonomous, and therefore able to navigate NHS maternity services and overcome any barriers to engagement. Furthermore, the 'ideal birthing citizen' is presumed to be white and to speak fluent English, reflecting racialized and raciolinguistic discourses around UK citizenship and belonging. Finally, and perhaps most importantly, the 'ideal birthing citizen' makes 'good choices' regarding maternity care, prioritizing her baby's health and safeguarding NHS services, and if she doesn't, her choices may be overruled. Women and other birthing people who fail to conform to the norm of the 'ideal birthing citizen' may be subject to substandard maternity care, or even obstetric violence.

Women's reproductive capacities tend to be foregrounded with regard to the role of the NHS in delineating the boundaries of national belonging. Early anxieties around the NHS and migration were heavily gendered; while concerns about male migrants tended to focus on disease, female migrants were seen as having 'too many babies' and exposing their children to ill health through 'bad mothering' (Bivins, 2015). As bordering processes have proliferated (discussed in more detail later), NHS bordering has similarly been justified, in part, with reference to the figure of the 'pregnant migrant' coming to the UK to illicitly use NHS maternity services.

Beyond maternity care, social citizenship more broadly is also informed by, and informs, discourses, policies, and practices around reproduction. This is reflected and reinforced in bordering processes around social citizenship, which serve to construct some migrants as more threatening to the national reproductive future than others, and to discipline migrants' reproductive practices according to these constructions. As discussed in both Chapters 1 and 4, the policies, services, and resources associated with social citizenship, like housing or access to an income, are especially critical to reproduction, and the structure and provision of these entitlements are underpinned by gendered, racialized, and classed discourses around who should be carrying out reproductive tasks, and how. Bordering around social citizenship contributes to the construction of different 'categories' of migrants as more or less 'desirable', and indicates what behaviour is expected of migrants, including with regard to reproduction. Migrants on work and family visas, for example, are expected to demonstrate 'responsible reproductive citizenship' – reproducing with minimal support from the state – in order to settle in the UK, but there is a clear route to settlement and building a family life, even if it is constrained.

By contrast, asylum seekers are barred from working and receive grossly inadequate income and housing from the state. Bordering processes around social citizenship send the message that these migrants are highly 'undesirable' and should not be reproducing *at all* (see also Lonergan, 2018).

Similarly, family bordering processes are intertwined with the construction of the heteronormative nuclear family as the 'legitimate site' of the reproduction of the nation state. Family bordering processes are informed by anxieties around reproduction and the ability of the migrant family to reproduce the nation state 'correctly'. At the same time, these bordering processes serve to discipline families with migrant members into conforming to the economically self-sufficient, autonomous, procreative couple norm – the current, dominant iteration of the heteronormative nuclear family model. While the heteronormative nuclear family is privileged above all other family forms in these processes, for migrants, the right to life in the UK with one's spouse and children is highly conditional and tied up with demonstrating one can be trusted to reproduce the nation state 'correctly'. This involves, first, in keeping with raciolinguistic discourses noted earlier, showing that one can speak English so as not to prevent the integration of one's future children, and second, demonstrating 'responsible reproductive citizenship' and the ability to reproduce without burdening the welfare state. Additionally, family bordering processes stratify access to support for reproduction from both the state and from extended family members. Conforming to the economically productive, procreative couple norm has become more difficult as bordering processes have become more intense. Even some of the relatively privileged migrants I interviewed discussed 'carrying the weight' of the uncertainty and stress produced by bordering processes, and the way it constrained their decisions around reproduction and family life.

Proliferating bordering processes

The proliferation of bordering processes has extended and strengthened the reach of the state in disciplining migrants' reproductive activities. These proliferating bordering processes are situated, in the sense that individuals experience them differently depending, first, on their location within intersecting social systems, including gender, race, and class, and second, on their role with regard to the specific bordering processes they encounter. They are also situated in that they are shaped by the particular site at which they are located. As I discussed in Chapter 4 especially, the political, institutional, and cultural specificities of different bordering sites may serve to shape, mediate, or even undermine the implementation and the effects of these processes. Moreover, as bordering processes multiply and proliferate, processes located at different sites interact with, reinforce, and occasionally undermine each other, producing a highly complex and variegated pattern of stratified reproduction, and also opening up new spaces of resistance and mediation.

Bordering processes associated with housing or income support reinforce the bordering of maternity services, making it more difficult for some migrants, especially asylum seekers, to access healthcare to which they are statutorily entitled. The resulting stratification is further variegated by the availability of local support, and individual migrants' material and social resources. Furthermore, the specificities of NHS maternity services as a bordering site sometimes serve to mediate both the bordering occurring within these services and the bordering processes associated with other aspects of social citizenship. Many of the NHS staff I interviewed believed that all pregnant people, regardless of immigration status, should be allowed to access maternity services free of charge. Some consequently 'forgot' to record a woman's status, or intervened with the Overseas Visitors Office where they felt a woman had been wrongly charged or to negotiate a minimal payment plan. Furthermore, sympathetic midwives and doctors also supported their patients in negotiating other aspects of the immigration system that might interfere with their maternal health, for example, helping asylum-seeking patients apply for a maternity grant from the Home Office or putting patients in touch with charities that could help them in acquiring necessities for their baby.

Nonetheless, there are limits to the potential for resistance and mediation that may open with the proliferation of bordering processes. As I discuss in more detail in the final section of this chapter, there is a limit to what medical professionals can do in compensating for the exclusions produced by bordering processes. Moreover, many health professionals are not attempting to undermine or resist bordering processes, whether from ignorance regarding the immigration system or from what Marie refers to in Chapter 4 as 'Daily Mail-y' views regarding pregnant migrants. Furthermore, additional sympathy for some pregnant migrants may stem from their construction as an especially vulnerable and therefore 'deserving' group. Deservingness is a highly contested and contingent category, however, one that is gendered, racialized, and classed, and constructed in relation to individual gatekeepers (Willen, 2012; Willen and Cook, 2016; Malakasis and Sahraoui, 2020; Sahraoui, 2021). Indeed, Willen and Cook (2016: 96) characterize health-related deservingness as 'the flip-side of rights'. Rather than providing universal access to maternity care, support for pregnant migrants based on 'deservingness' is not only unreliable, but serves to further stratify reproduction according to the sympathies of individual healthcare workers and whether a particular migrant is perceived as 'deserving'.

Further considerations

'Choice' in maternity care through the lens of reproductive justice

The reproductive justice framework offers an important challenge to current discourses around 'choice' in childbirth and the exclusions they can produce with regard to maternity care.[1] As discussed in the Introduction, reproductive justice activists problematize liberal individualist notions of 'choice'. The framework applies a human rights lens to questions of reproduction, exploring how interacting discourses, policies, and institutions differentially distribute the resources required for genuine reproductive autonomy while also constructing the reproductive practices of certain individuals and groups as 'undesirable' or even 'threatening'. Reproductive justice understands individuals making decisions around childbirth within wider discursive, cultural, and material contexts that limit the options realistically available to them, and constrain their choices.

By the 1960s in the UK, childbirth had become heavily medicalized and 'responsible reproductive citizenship' for women consisted of submitting oneself to the 'expertise' of medical professionals, regardless of one's personal preferences (Davis, 2012; McIntosh, 2012; Oakley, 2016). As discussed in Chapter 5, since then, there has been a striking evolution with regard to women's rights and responsibilities in childbirth. Campaigning by feminists and patients' rights activists, and the advent of neoliberal models of citizenship emphasizing personal responsibility and self-sufficiency, have resulted in an expectation that women be actively involved in making decisions around their care in pregnancy and childbirth. Indeed, the words 'choice' or 'choices' appear 74 times in *Better Births* (National Maternity Review, 2016).

However, this emphasis on 'patient choices' has been something of a double-edged sword for women and other birthing people. On the one hand, the acknowledgement that women 'should' have a say in their care is a significant advance over the expectation that they submit to the wishes of medical professionals. Moreover, it is important to recognize that discourses around 'choice' in childbirth are materialized in the actions of individual medical staff and mediated by their interpretation of what this means. Many of my participants, as I noted in Chapter 5, felt that their midwife had respected their preferences. On the other hand, the acknowledgement that women should have a choice has been accompanied by the expectation that they make 'good choices', where 'good' reflects both (contested) medical consensus and wider discourses around 'responsible reproductive citizenship' and the behaviour desired in individuals responsible for reproducing the nation state. This includes, as Lowe (2016) argues, the obligation to subsume one's own preferences for what is 'best for the baby', in keeping with an 'ethos of sacrifice'. Where women fail to make 'good choices', some medical professionals feel entitled to disregard their preferences, or pressure them into making different choices. This disregard for women's preferences likely has multiple causes, which are not reducible to discourses and expectations around 'responsible reproductive citizenship'; nevertheless, these discourses and expectations are an important element of the wider context in which such disregard is occurring. Furthermore, in keeping with the construction of the 'responsible reproductive citizen' as autonomous and self-sufficient, as well as raciolinguistic discourses associating fluency in English with belonging, barriers to engaging with maternity services, and making and enacting 'good' choices, are largely ignored within *Better Births* (National Maternity Review, 2016), as well as sometimes in practice.

Through the lens of reproductive justice, however, women and other birthing people are entitled to bodily autonomy, and to make decisions around pregnancy, childbirth, and maternity care, because they are *human* and bodily autonomy is a *human right*. 'Choice' in childbirth is therefore detached from the expectation that individuals make 'good' choices, whether to ensure the 'correct' reproduction of the nation state, to safeguard the health of the foetus, or to improve NHS services. Similarly, a reproductive justice approach illuminates that 'choice' with regard to maternity care is meaningless if you are too distressed and preoccupied with trying to regularize your immigration status to attend appointments; or cannot afford the bus fare to the maternity clinic; or have been abruptly dispersed to a new city and don't have a GP yet; or cannot read the language of the informational pamphlets you have been given; or aren't sure what your options are with regard to care. A focus on reproductive justice and reproductive autonomy, rather than choices, maintains that women and other birthing people should have the right to make all decisions with regard to their care, and asks us what conditions need to be in place to actualize this.

Precarious pregnant migrants as 'disposable subjects'

The reproductive justice lens also highlights the extent to which pregnant migrants with a precarious immigration status are constructed within discourses and policies around citizenship and reproduction as 'disposable' subjects (Giroux, 2006). Even those pregnant migrants who are relatively privileged – white, middle class, English-speaking, with a relatively stable immigration status – may experience reproductive injustice and stratified reproduction as a consequence of bordering processes, as well as difficulties conforming to the norm of the 'ideal birthing citizen'. Emily, a white North American, discussed how maintaining a secure immigration status influenced her decisions around becoming pregnant (Chapter 3) and her difficulties navigating the NHS as an immigrant (Chapter 5). However, there is an especially noticeable, and striking, disjuncture between the rights and responsibilities of the 'ideal birthing citizen' and the treatment of pregnant migrants with a precarious status. By this I mean a migrant whose right to stay in the country is uncertain, whether because they are un(der)documented, an asylum seeker, or 'refused' asylum seeker, or in the middle of some other dispute related to their visa. This precarious immigration status locates these migrants as 'undesirable' and 'unwanted' within the UK, contrasted with migrants who are potentially acceptable future citizens.[2] As such, they are constructed as unsuited to reproduce the nation state; indeed, their reproductive practices may be seen as inherently threatening to the national future. They are provided with very limited or no support from the state, and may be discouraged from reproducing. In short, they are constructed as 'disposable, an unnecessary burden on state coffers ... consigned to fend for themselves' (Giroux, 2006: 174; see also Lonergan, 2024b).

This is exemplified by the decision, discussed in Chapter 2, to proceed with charging pregnant people for maternity care under the Immigration Act 2014, even though the Home Office (2013b) and the Department of Health (2013a; 2013c) acknowledged that severe harm to pregnant people could be caused by the charging regime. Pregnant migrants' perceived 'vulnerability' was used perversely to reinforce the claim that they posed a potential threat to the UK; they and their children were so undesirable that it was deemed acceptable to expose them to severe harm, and even death, in order to save 0.018 per cent of the NHS budget. The practice of charging birthing migrants for maternity care persists despite the 2019 MBRRACE-UK report (Knight et al, 2019) linking three maternal deaths to the regime.

The disjuncture between the 'ideal birthing citizen' and the disposability of pregnant migrants is visible in other ways. *Better Births* (National Maternity Review, 2016) repeatedly stresses the importance of 'continuity of carer' in ensuring the best outcomes for birthing parents and babies; yet, the dispersal of pregnant migrants continues, despite the disruption this causes to continuity of carer. Indeed, although Home Office regulations theoretically forbid dispersing asylum seekers after 34 weeks of pregnancy, the practice nonetheless persists, as happened to Sana (see Chapter 4). Precarious pregnant migrants are entitled to very little state support, but even this is often withheld due to 'mistakes' by gatekeepers and bureaucratic foot-dragging on the part of the Home Office and its agents. Examples include Elior, told to 'be patient' as she was forced to spend her pregnancy in a one-bedroom flat with two children in the middle of a pandemic, and Migrant Help took months to resolve its own error; or Humaira, housed while pregnant in a hotel room and doing her two other children's laundry in the sink, and then told she had to move out the day she returned from giving birth in hospital. At the post-project workshop, one of the participants recounted watching the representative of the company that managed the asylum housing in which she was living count off the *exact* number of nappies that another resident with a new baby was entitled to, rather than simply giving her the box. The constructed 'disposability' of precarious pregnant migrants and new parents exists at the structural, institutional, and individual scale. While all birthing people are entitled to reproductive justice, the situation of precarious migrants is especially shocking and must be addressed urgently.

Reproductive justice for pregnant and birthing migrants and new parents

As discussed in Chapter 4, knowledgeable and sympathetic NHS staff can make a significant difference to the health and experiences of individual migrants. Some of my asylum-seeking interviewees, in particular, spoke in glowing terms of their midwife and the additional support she had offered in securing a maternity grant and/or adequate housing, or in checking whether they had enough food in the house. Furthermore, the Royal College of Midwives (2021a) and the Royal College of Obstetricians and Gynaecologists (n.d.) have published guidelines for caring for vulnerable migrants that clearly indicate an awareness that the 'ideal birthing citizen' of *Better Births* is unrepresentative and exclusionary. Recommendations include using professional interpreters who are not related to the patient (Royal College of Obstetricians and Gynaecologists, n.d.; Royal College of Midwives, 2021a) and being aware that travel costs may be an obstacle to attending appointments (Royal College of Midwives, 2021a). Yet, amid severe funding and staffing crises within the NHS, how much more can be expected of midwives and other healthcare professionals? The use of an interpreter where necessary should be standard, but is it reasonable to ask midwives to develop the knowledge required to support patients in navigating the asylum system? Similarly, many third sector organizations provide important emotional and practical support to precarious pregnant migrants, but they are also under severe pressure due to austerity and the high cost of remaining open. Moreover, often (but not always) they are mainly addressing the symptoms of the exclusions produced by bordering processes and inadequacies within maternity services, rather than the underlying causes.

Reproductive justice for migrants is impossible in a world with bordering processes, and the gendered and racialized exclusionary discourses that underpin them. Even the relatively privileged migrants I interviewed discussed the way their reproductive choices, and the support available to them, were shaped by bordering processes; for the more precarious migrants, as discussed earlier, these processes meant trying to survive pregnancy and childbirth and raise children in conditions that were grossly inadequate. If some people are excluded from the national community, their reproductive practices will be considered threatening, and they will be denied the rights and resources they require for genuine reproductive autonomy.

Recommendations

The abolition of immigration controls, a welfare state that provides necessary resources for reproductive autonomy to all residents of the UK, racial justice within maternity services, and a fully funded NHS available free of charge to anyone who needs it

While I am realistic about how likely it is that any of the above will be accomplished soon, I think it is important to put into writing what is actually required for reproductive justice for migrants, and indeed, many UK citizens.

More immediately achievable recommendations

An end to charging for NHS maternity care

The Royal College of Midwives (2022b) and the Royal College of Obstetricians and Gynaecologists (n.d.) have both called for an end to charging eligible migrants for maternity care. As outlined earlier, the actual 'cost' of un(der)documented pregnant migrants to the NHS is a tiny fraction of the overall budget, but the implementation of charges has cost lives. Providing maternity care, free of charge, to anyone who requires it is very achievable.

Implementation of the recommendations made by FiveXMore (Peter et al, 2022) and Birthrights (2022) to address individual and institutional racism within maternity services

Many migrants are racialized as white, and most racially minoritized people affected by racism within maternity services are citizens. Nonetheless, racism negatively impacts racially minoritized migrants' experiences of maternity care. Moreover, because migration is a heavily racialized issue within the UK, the association between 'migrant' and 'racially minoritized' in the popular imagination may make migrants especially vulnerable to racism in maternity services.

Respect for patients' bodily autonomy

While midwives and other medical staff can inform patients regarding current consensus around the best options in medical care, they should ultimately respect whatever decision a birthing patient makes. They should also be aware that migrant patients especially may be used to different norms around 'best practice' and be able to communicate the reasoning behind standard NHS practices.

Use of professional interpreters in all healthcare settings

Again, this is already recommended by professional associations but is not implemented in practice. Materials should also be available in a wide range of languages, and it should be possible to access recordings of informational material being read in a wide range of languages, for those pregnant people who don't read their first language.

Establishment of specialist maternity services and expansion of their remit

Every trust should have specialist maternity services for migrant patients, with midwives who are able to take on the additional challenge of addressing the barriers to a healthy pregnancy facing these patients. Given the additional workload, these midwives may have a reduced number of birthing people in their care. Furthermore, existing services tend to be offered to those migrants perceived as especially 'vulnerable', for example, asylum seekers or very recent arrivals. The remit should be expanded, with migrant patients being informed of the services available and being allowed to 'opt-in' if they feel it would benefit them.

Trusts to be provided with funding to support pregnant people struggling to attend antenatal, perinatal, and postnatal appointments

As discussed in Chapter 4, precarious migrants may struggle to attend medical appointments because of travel costs, caring responsibilities, or the stress of navigating the immigration system. Funding that could be used to pay their travel costs *at the time of the appointment*, or pay for childcare, might make this easier for some pregnant migrants, and indeed, the many British citizens living in poverty.

Recognition that even privileged migrants may struggle with navigating the NHS

Migrant women who do not feel they need specialist services may still be unsure regarding the organization and provision of NHS maternity services and their entitlements, or why certain treatments are considered preferable. Midwives and other NHS staff should be prepared to provide information about this, and again, there may be British citizens who also find NHS maternity services confusing and would benefit from this.

Notes

Chapter 1

[1] Although this was arguably implied by both the use of an antisemitic allusion and the naming of immigration as a problem.

[2] The US Supreme Court decision recognizing a limited right to abortion.

[3] Although place of birth and/or citizenship is not always recorded for birthing people (Bunch and Knight, 2023).

[4] Since the 1990s there has been increasing interest among social scientists regarding citizenship at other scales, notably transnational and local citizenships (see Isin, 2002; Soysal, 2012).

[5] Several scholars have pointed out that in practice, the implementation of neoliberal economic restructuring tends to require significant state intervention, both to quash opposition and to create the conditions necessary to maximize corporate profits (Brenner and Theodore, 2002).

[6] No political party achieved an overall majority of seats in the House of Commons in the 2010 UK election, so the Conservative and Liberal Democrat parties formed a coalition government, which lasted until 2015.

[7] State benefit for unemployed people or those in low-paid work.

[8] There are some exceptions, including for multiple births, adoptees, and where a child is born as the result of rape (Gov.uk, 2021).

[9] Interestingly, it can also be read as the state conceding that citizens do have a right to a limited family life, including one or two children.

[10] This eventually culminated in the 2005 referendum that voted to abolish *jus soli* citizenship in Ireland (Luibhéid, 2013).

Chapter 2

[1] With the notable exception of the US.

[2] This was prior to the UK's decision to leave the EU; migrants from the EU are now also required to pay the IHS.

[3] Although, as Allen et al (2017) point out, it is also expected that different NHS bodies and providers will cooperate with each other to ensure the best care for patients.

[4] The King's Fund is an 'independent charitable organization working to improve health and care in England' (kingsfund.org).

Chapter 3

[1] An exception can be made where an individual is coming to live with a relative in the UK so that said relative can provide them with long-term necessary care they cannot get in their country of origin (Gov.uk, n.d.-b).

[2] Increasing if one wished also to sponsor children (Home Office, 2012).

[3] The use of English language requirements in the construction of racialized borders is taken up in more detail in Chapter 5.

[4] This visa scheme is no longer in place.

[5] For the most part throughout this book, I refer to participants' region of origin, rather than a specific country, in order to better safeguard anonymity. I have opted to name participants' country of origin in this section because it is directly relevant to their experiences of relatives being unable to visit, as citizens of Syria and Libya in particular were considered at risk of 'overstaying' due to the conflicts in both countries.

[6] There is a much wider literature exploring resistance and agency, including discussion around Katz's framing (for an excellent summary, see Hughes, 2020; Hughes et al, 2022); however, to fully do justice to this literature is beyond the scope of this book. Katz's framing is useful for the reasons discussed, and her use of resilience, and interest in the relationship between resilience and more explicit oppositional activities, has parallels with Patricia Hill Collins' (2000) emphasis on individual and community survival as foundational to black women's activism (see also Bassel and Emejulu, 2017).

Chapter 4

[1] In theory, asylum seekers may take up jobs on the Shortage Occupation List if they have been waiting 12 months or more for a decision on their case (Gower et al, 2022), but in practice, it is extremely unusual for an asylum seeker to be granted the right to work.

[2] Asylum support rates from 2020 and 2022 can be viewed on the Wayback Machine hosted by the Internet Archive: https://web.archive.org/web/20201128112650/https://www.gov.uk/asylum-support/what-youll-get (November 2020); https://web.archive.org/web/20220812094557/https://www.gov.uk/asylum-support/what-youll-get (August 2022).

[3] The implications of financial dependency upon one's spouse are discussed in Chapter 3.

[4] The charity contracted by the Home Office to manage asylum support.

Chapter 5

[1] It is beyond the scope of this book to rehearse the debates around 'medicalized' and 'natural' childbirth; see Treichler (1990); Beckett (2005); and Brubaker and Dillaway (2008) for helpful summaries.

[2] The second report from the House of Commons Social Services Committee on Perinatal and Neonatal Mortality (Parliament. House of Commons, 1980).

[3] The emphasis on family is discussed more in Chapter 3.

[4] Both historically and at present, discourses constructing white working-class people, especially the 'underclass', as inferior and problematic have drawn on their supposed cultural and geographic proximity to racially minoritized people, especially black people (see McClintock, 1995; Tyler, 2008).

[5] I distinctly remember being told at NHS antenatal classes I attended while pregnant that there was no reason to fear the pain of childbirth because African women give birth in fields every day.

[6] A US government program that covers the costs of medical care for individuals with very low incomes.

[7] I am indebted on this point to Laura Sochas.

[8] As discussed in Chapter 3, many of the married women I interviewed cited their husbands as especially important sources of emotional and practical support.

Chapter 6

[1] The reflections underpinning this section were prompted by an incisive question asked by Rishita Nandagiri at the Reproductive Justice Now! Conference in London on 8–9 May 2024.

[2] Even as un(der)documented migrants are positioned as a reserve army of easily exploitable labour on which the economy depends (De Genova, 2010a; Mezzadra and Nielsen, 2013).

References

Abji S and Larios L (2021) Migrant justice as reproductive justice: birthright citizenship and the politics of immigration detention for pregnant women in Canada. *Citizenship Studies* 25(2): 253–272.

Aldred R (2008) NHS LIFT and the new shape of neoliberal welfare. *Capital & Class* 32(2): 31–57.

Aliverti A (2015) Enlisting the public in the policing of immigration. *British Journal of Criminology* 55(2): 215–230.

All-Party Parliamentary Group on Birth Trauma (2024) *Listen to Mums: Ending the Postcode Lottery on Perinatal Care*. Available at: https://www.theo-clarke.org.uk/birth-trauma-report (accessed 13 June 2024).

Allen P, Osipovič D, Shepherd E, Coleman A, Perkins N, Garnett E, et al (2017) Commissioning through competition and cooperation in the English NHS under the Health and Social Care Act 2012: Evidence from a qualitative study of four clinical commissioning groups. *BMJ Open* 7(2): e011745.

Amos V and Parmar P (1984) Challenging imperial feminism. *Feminist Review* 17(1): 3–19.

Anandaciva S (2024) *The Spring Budget 2024: What does it mean for health and care services?* Available at: https://www.kingsfund.org.uk/insight-and-analysis/blogs/spring-budget-2024-health-care-services (accessed 27 January 2025).

Anandaciva S and Ward D (2019) *How is the NHS performing? July 2019 quarterly monitoring report*. Available at: https://www.kingsfund.org.uk/insight-and-analysis/reports/how-nhs-performing-july-2019 (accessed 19 March 2024).

Anderson B (2013) *Us and Them? The Dangerous Politics of Immigration Control* (online edn). Oxford University Press.

Andrijasevic R (2009) Sex on the move: Gender, subjectivity and differential inclusion. *Subjectivity* 29(1): 389–506.

Anitha S (2008) Neither safety nor justice: The UK government response to domestic violence against immigrant women. *Journal of Social Welfare and Family Law* 30(3): 189–202.

Aquino MRJV, Edge D, and Smith DM (2015) Pregnancy as an ideal time for intervention to address the complex needs of black and minority ethnic women: Views of British midwives. *Midwifery* 31(3): 373–379.

Arcilla JT, Nanou A, Hamed S, and Osman F (2025) Racialized migrant women's discrimination in maternal care: a scoping review. *International Journal for Equity in Health* 24(1): 16.

Baggott R (2016) Health policy and the coalition government. In: Bochel H and Powell M (eds) *The Coalition Government and Social Policy: Restructuring the Welfare State.* Bristol: Policy Press, pp 99–126.

Bambra C and Garthwaite K (2015) Austerity, welfare reform and the English health divide. *Area* 47(3): 341–343.

Barton N (2020) *Reproductive Citizens: Gender, Immigration, and the State in Modern France, 1880–1945.* Ithaca, NY: Cornell University Press.

Bassel L and Emejulu A (2017) *Minority Women and Austerity: Survival and Resistance in France and Britain.* Bristol; Chicago: Policy Press.

Bassel L and Khan K (2021) Migrant women becoming British citizens: Care and coloniality. *Citizenship Studies* 25(4): 583–601.

Beckett K (2005) Choosing cesarean: Feminism and the politics of childbirth in the United States. *Feminist Theory* 6(3): 251–275.

Benhabib S (2004) *The Rights of Others: Aliens, Residents and Citizens.* Cambridge; New York; Port Melbourne; Madrid; Cape Town: Cambridge University Press.

Bevan G, Karanikolos M, Exley J, Nolte E, Connolly S, and Mays N (2014) *The Four Health Systems of the UK: How Do They Compare?* London: The Health Foundation and Nuffield Trust.

Beynon-Jones SM (2013) Expecting motherhood? Stratifying reproduction in 21st-century Scottish abortion practice. *Sociology* 47(3): 509–525.

Bhattacharyya G (2015) *Crisis, Austerity, and Everyday Life: Living in a Time of Diminishing Expectations.* Basingstoke; New York: Palgrave Macmillan.

Bhavnani K-K and Coulson M (1986) Transforming socialist-feminism: the challenge of racism. *Feminist Review* 23(1): 81–92.

Birthrights (2018) *Maternal Request Caesarean.* London: Birthrights.

Birthrights (2022) *Systemic Racism, Not Broken Bodies: An Inquiry into Racial Injustice and Human Rights in UK Maternity Care.* London: Birthrights.

Bivins RE (2015) *Contagious Communities: Medicine, Migration, and the NHS in Post-war Britain.* Oxford; New York: Oxford University Press.

Bloch A (2000) A new era or more of the same? Asylum policy in the UK. *Journal of Refugee Studies* 13(1): 29–42.

Bloch A (2013) The labour market experiences and strategies of young undocumented migrants. *Work, Employment and Society* 27(2): 272–287.

Bloch A and Schuster L (2005) Asylum policy under new labour. *Benefits: A Journal of Poverty and Social Justice* 13(2): 115–118.

Block ES and Erskine L (2012) Interviewing by telephone: Specific considerations, opportunities, and challenges. *International Journal of Qualitative Methods* 11(4): 428–445.

Bond Leonard TM (2017) Laying the Foundations for a Reproductive Justice Movement. In: Ross LJ, Roberts L, Derkas E, Peoples W, and Bridgewater Toure P (eds) *Radical Reproductive Justice: Foundations, Theory, Practice, Critique.* New York: Feminist Press at CUNY.

Bonizzoni P (2011) Civic stratification, stratified reproduction and family solidarity: Strategies of Latino families in Milan. In: Kraler A, Kofman E, Kohli M, and Schmoll C (eds) *Gender, Generations and the Family in International Migration.* Amsterdam: Amsterdam University Press, pp 313–334.

Borchorst A and Siim B (1987) Women and the advanced welfare state: a new kind of patriarchal power? In: Sassoon AS (ed) *Women and the State.* London; Melbourne; Sidney; Auckland; Johannesburg: Hutchinson Education, pp 128–157.

Bragg B and Wong LL (2016) 'Cancelled dreams': Family reunification and shifting Canadian immigration policy. *Journal of Immigrant & Refugee Studies* 14(1): 46–65.

Brenner N and Theodore N (2002) Cities and the geographies of 'actually existing neoliberalism'. In: Brenner N and Theodore N (eds) *Spaces of Neoliberalism: Urban Restructuring in North America and Western Europe.* Malden, MA; Oxford; Victoria: Blackwell Publishers Ltd, pp 1–32.

Bridges KM (2011) *Reproducing Race: An Ethnography of Pregnancy as a Site of Racialization.* Berkeley and Los Angeles; London: University of California Press.

Brookes G (2021) Empowering people to make healthier choices: a critical discourse analysis of the tackling obesity policy. *Qualitative Health Research* 31(12): 2211–2229.

Brown BJ and Baker S (2012) *Responsible Citizens: Individuals, Health, and Policy Under Neoliberalism.* London; New York: Anthem Press.

Brown W (2005) *Edgework: Critical Essays on Knowledge and Politics.* Princeton, NJ; Oxford: Princeton University Press.

Brown W (2015) *Undoing the Demos: Neoliberalism's Stealth Revolution.* Brooklyn, NY: Zone Books.

Browne V (2016) 'The money follows the mum': Maternal power as consumer power. *Radical Philosophy* 199.

Brubaker SJ and Dillaway HE (2008) Re-examining the meanings of childbirth: Beyond gender and the 'natural' versus 'medical' dichotomy. In: Texler Segal M and Demos V (eds) *Advancing Gender Research from the Nineteenth to the Twenty-first Centuries.* Bingley, BD: Emerald Group Publishing Limited, pp 217–244.

Bryan B, Dadzie S, and Scafe S (2018) *The Heart of the Race: Black Women's Lives in Britain.* London: Verso Books.

Bunch K and Knight M (2023) Maternal Mortality in the UK 2019–21: Surveillance and Epidemiology. In: Knight M, Bunch K, Felker A, Patel R, Kotnis R, Kenyon S, et al (eds) *Saving Lives, Improving Mothers' Care: Lessons Learned to Inform Maternity Care from the UK and Ireland Confidential Enquiries into Maternal Deaths and Morbidity 2019–21.* Oxford: National Perinatal Epidemiology Unit, University of Oxford.

Burman E and Chantler K (2005) Domestic violence and minoritisation: Legal and policy barriers facing minoritized women leaving violent relationships. *International Journal of Law and Psychiatry* 28(1): 59–74.

Burnett J (2004) Community, cohesion and the state. *Race & Class* 45(3): 1–18.

Bussemaker J (2005) Introduction: An ethnographic portrait of a precarious life: getting by on even less. In: Bussemaker J (ed) *Citizenship and Welfare State Reform in Europe.* London; New York: Routledge, Taylor & Francis, pp 1–11.

Byrne B (2006) *White Lives: The Interplay of 'Race', Class and Gender in Everyday Life.* Abingdon, Oxon; New York: Routledge.

Byrne B (2015) Rethinking intersectionality and whiteness at the borders of citizenship. *Sociological Research Online* 20(3): 178–189.

Cairns K and Johnston J (2015) Choosing health: Embodied neoliberalism, postfeminism, and the 'do-diet'. *Theory and Society* 44: 153–175.

Campbell C (2021) Medical violence, obstetric racism, and the limits of informed consent for Black women. *Michigan Journal of Race & Law* 47.

Carroll K and Kroløkke C (2018) Freezing for love: enacting 'responsible' reproductive citizenship through egg freezing. *Culture, Health & Sexuality* 20(9): 992–1005.

Cassidy K (2018) Everyday bordering, healthcare and the politics of belonging in contemporary Britain. In: Paasi A, Prokkola E-K, Saarinen J, and Zimmerbauer K (eds) *Borderless Worlds for Whom? Ethics, Moralities and Mobilities.* Abingdon, Oxon: Routledge.

Cassidy K, Amiri R, and Davidson J (2023) Reading for refusal in UK maternity care: entangling struggles for border and reproductive justice. *Fennia-International Journal of Geography* 201(2): 200–214.

Castañeda H (2008) Paternity for sale: anxieties over 'demographic theft' and undocumented migrant reproduction in Germany. *Medical Anthropology Quarterly* 22(4): 340–359.

Cates M (2013) *Our declining birth rate.* Available at: https://www.miriamcates.org.uk/news/our-declining-birth-rate (accessed 17 May 2024).

Centre for Health and Public Interest (2023) *P.F.I. Profiting from inflation? Understanding the impact of inflation on the affordability of NHS PFI contracts.* London: Centre for Health and Public Interest.

Chadwick R (2021) Breaking the frame: Obstetric violence and epistemic rupture. *Agenda* 35(3): 104–115.

Cisneros N (2013) 'Alien' sexuality: Race, maternity, and citizenship. *Hypatia* 28(2): 290–306.

Clarke A (2021) Recognising British bodies: The significance of race and whiteness in 'post-racial' Britain. *Sociological Research Online* 28(1): 279–295.

Coddington K (2020) Incompatible with life: Embodied borders, migrant fertility, and the UK's 'hostile environment'. *Environment and Planning C: Politics and Space* 39(8): 1711–1724.

Cohen S (1985) Anti-semitism, immigration controls and the welfare state. *Critical Social Policy* 5(13): 73–92.

Colen S (1995) 'Like a mother to them': Stratified reproduction and West Indian childcare workers and employers in New York. In: Ginsburg FD and Rapp R (eds) *Conceiving the New World Order: The Global Politics of Reproduction*. Berkeley; Los Angeles; London: University of California Press, pp 73–102.

Collins PH (1998) It's all in the family: Intersections of gender, race, and nation. *Hypatia* 13(3): 62–82.

Collins PH (2000) *Black Feminist Thought: Knowledge, Consciousness, and the Politics of Empowerment*. London; New York: Routledge.

Combahee River Collective (1977/1981) A black feminist statement. In: Moraga C and Anzaldùa G (eds) *This Bridge Called My Back: Writings by Radical Women of Color*. Watertown, MA: Persephone Press.

Crawford R (1980) Healthism and the medicalization of everyday life. *International Journal of Health Services* 10(3): 365–388.

Crawford R (2006) Health as a meaningful social practice. *Health: An Interdisciplinary Journal for the Social Study of Health, Illness and Medicine* 10(4): 401–420.

Crawshaw P (2013) Public health policy and the behavioural turn: The case of social marketing. *Critical Social Policy* 33(4): 616–637.

Creative Research (2013) *Qualitative assessment of visitor and migrant use of the NHS in England: Observations from the front line*. London: Department of Health.

Cribb A (2008) Organizational reform and health-care goods: concerns about marketization in the UK NHS. *Journal of Medicine and Philosophy* 33(3): 221–240.

d'Aoust A-M (2018) A moral economy of suspicion: Love and marriage migration management practices in the United Kingdom. *Environment and Planning D: Society and Space* 36(1): 40–59.

Darling J (2022) *Systems of Suffering: Dispersal and the Denial of Asylum*. London: Pluto Press.

Davies AC (2013) This time, it's for real: the Health and Social Care Act 2012. *The Modern Law Review* 76(3): 564–588.

Davin A (1978) Imperialism and motherhood. *History Workshop Journal* 5(1): 9–66.

Davis A (2012) *Modern Motherhood: Women and family in England, 1945–2000*. Manchester; New York: Manchester University Press.

Davis AY (1981) *Women, Race & Class*. New York: Random House.

Davis D-A (2009) The Politics of Reproduction: The Troubling Case of Nadya Suleman and Assisted Reproductive Technology[*]. *Transforming Anthropology* 17(2): 105–116.

Davis D-A (2019a) Obstetric racism: the racial politics of pregnancy, labor, and birthing. *Medical Anthropology* 38(7): 560–573.

Davis D-A (2019b) *Reproductive Injustice: Racism, Pregnancy, and Premature Birth*. New York: New York University Press.

de Benedictis S (2012) Feral parents: austerity parenting under neoliberalism. *Studies in the Maternal*, 4(2): 1–21.

De Genova N (2010a) The deportation regime: Sovereignty, space, and the freedom of movement. In: Genova ND and Peutz N (eds) *The Deportation Regime: Sovereignty, Space, and the Freedom of Movement*. Durham, NC; London: Duke University Press.

De Genova N (2010b) The queer politics of migration: Reflections on 'illegality' and incorrigibility. *Studies in Social Justice* 4(2): 101–126.

De Noronha L (2022) Hierarchies of membership and the management of global population: reflections on citizenship and racial ordering. *Citizenship Studies* 26(4–5): 426–435.

De Vries R, Benoit C, Van Teijlingen E, and Wrede S (eds) (2002a) *Birth by Design: Pregnancy, Maternity Care and Midwifery in North America and Europe*. New York; London: Routledge.

De Vries R, Benoit C, Van Teijlingen E, and Wrede S (2002b) Introduction: Why maternity care is *not* medical care. In: De Vries R, Benoit C, Van Teijlingen E, and Wrede S (eds) *Birth by Design: Pregnancy, Maternity Care and Midwifery in North America and Europe*. New York; London: Routledge, pp xi–xviii.

Deakin H and Wakefield K (2014) Skype interviewing: Reflections of two PhD researchers. *Qualitative Research* 14(5): 603–616.

Deave T, Johnson D, and Ingram J (2008) Transition to parenthood: the needs of parents in pregnancy and early parenthood. *BMC Pregnancy and Childbirth* 8: 1–11.

Department of Health (2009) *The NHS Constitution for England*. London: Department of Health.

Department of Health (2013a) Equality analysis. Sustaining services, ensuring fairness: Government response to the consultation on migrant access and financial contribution to NHS provision in England. London: Department of Health.

Department of Health (2013b) Sustaining services, ensuring fairness: A consultation on migrant access and their financial contribution to NHS provision in England. London: Department of Health.

Department of Health (2013c) Sustaining services, ensuring fairness: Government response to the consultation on migrant access and financial contribution to NHS provision in England. London: Department of Health.

Department of Health (2014) Visitor and migrant NHS cost recovery programme. London: Department of Health.

Department of Health and Social Care (2024) NHS cost recovery – overseas visitors. London: Department of Health and Social Care.

Department for Education (2023) *Childcare and early years survey of parents.* Available at: https://explore-education-statistics.service.gov.uk/find-statist ics/childcare-and-early-years-survey-of-parents (accessed 05 May 2024).

Dixon A, Robertson R, Appleby J, Burge P, Devlin N, and Magee H (2010) *Patient Choice: How Patients Choose and How Providers Respond.* London: The King's Fund.

Doctors of the World (2018) *Submission to PHE call for evidence on data-sharing MoU between NHS Digital and Home Office.* London: Doctors of the World.

Douglass C and Lokugamage A (2021) Racial profiling for induction of labour: Improving safety or perpetuating racism? *BMJ* 375(2652): 1–2.

Dudley RG (2017) Domestic abuse and women with 'no recourse to public funds': The state's role in shaping and reinforcing coercive control. *Families, Relationships and Societies* 6(2): 201–217.

Dwyer P (2010) *Understanding Social Citizenship: Themes and Perspectives for Policy and Practice.* Bristol; Portland OR: Policy press.

El-Enany N (2020) *(B ordering Britain: Law, Race and Empire.* Manchester: Manchester University Press.

Erel U (2011) Reframing migrant mothers as citizens. *Citizenship Studies* 15(6–7): 695–709.

Erel U (2018) Saving and reproducing the nation: Struggles around right-wing politics of social reproduction, gender and race in austerity Europe. *Women's Studies International Forum* 68: 173–182.

Eslier M, Azria E, Chatzistergiou K, Stewart Z, Deschartres A, and Deneux-Tharaux C (2023) Association between migration and severe maternal outcomes in high-income countries: Systematic review and meta-analysis. *PLoS Medicine* 20(6): e1004257.

Fair F, Raben L, Watson H, Vivilaki V, van den Muijsenbergh M, Soltani H, et al (2020) Migrant women's experiences of pregnancy, childbirth and maternity care in European countries: A systematic review. *PloS One* 15(2): e0228378.

Feldman R (2013) *When maternity doesn't matter: Dispersing pregnant women seeking asylum.* London: Maternity Action and the Refugee Council.

Feldman R (2017) *The impact on health inequalities of charging migrant women for NHS maternity care: A scoping study.* London: Maternity Action.

Feldman R (2021) NHS charging for maternity care in England: Its impact on migrant women. *Critical Social Policy* 41(3): 447–467.

Feldman R, Hardwick J and Cleaver Malzoni R (2019) *Duty of Care? The impact on midwives of NHS charging for maternity care*. London: Maternity Action.

Feminist Fightback C (2011) Cuts are a feminist issue. *Soundings* 49: 73–84.

Firdous T, Darwin Z, and Hassan SM (2020) Muslim women's experiences of maternity services in the UK: Qualitative systematic review and thematic synthesis. *BMC Pregnancy and Childbirth* 20: 1–10.

Fortier AM (2010) Proximity by design? Affective citizenship and the management of unease. *Citizenship Studies* 14(1): 17–30.

Fortier AM (2021) *Uncertain Citizenship: Life in the Waiting Room*. Manchester: Manchester University Press.

Fox B and Worts D (1999) Revisiting the critique of medicalized childbirth: A contribution to the sociology of birth. *Gender & Society* 13(3): 326–346.

Francisco V (2015) 'The internet is magic': Technology, intimacy and transnational families. *Critical Sociology* 41(1): 173–190.

Fraser N (2016) Contradictions of Capital and Care. *New Left Review* 100: 99–117.

Gainsbury S (2023) *NHS spending plans and reality over the last 10 years*. Available at: https://www.nuffieldtrust.org.uk/resource/nhs-spending-plans-and-reality-over-the-past-10-years (accessed 19 March 2024).

Garcia R, Ali N, Papadopoulos C, and Randhawa G (2015) Specific antenatal interventions for Black, Asian and Minority Ethnic (BAME) pregnant women at high risk of poor birth outcomes in the United Kingdom: A scoping review. *BMC Pregnancy and Childbirth* 15: 1–13.

Gedalof I (2007) Unhomely homes: Women, family and belonging in UK discourses of migration and asylum. *Journal of Ethnic and Migration Studies* 33(1): 77–94.

Gilligan A (2013) The 300 'maternity tourists': Women cheating their way into UK to give birth for free. *The Telegraph Online*. Available at: https://www.telegraph.co.uk/news/uknews/immigration/10540881/The-300-maternity-tourists.html (accessed 27 January 2025).

Gilroy P (1987) *'There Ain't No Black in the Union Jack': The Cultural Politics of Race and Nation*. London: Hutchinson.

Ginsburg FD and Rapp R (1995) Introduction: Conceiving the new world order. In: Ginsburg FD and Rapp R (eds) *Conceiving the New World Order: The Global Politics of Reproduction*. Berkeley; Los Angeles; London: University of California Press, pp 1–17.

Giroux HA (2006) Reading Hurricane Katrina: Race, class, and the biopolitics of disposability. *College Literature* 33(3): 171–196.

Glenn EN (2011) Constructing citizenship: Exclusion, subordination, and resistance. *American Sociological Review* 76(1): 1–24.

GMCA Research (2023) *Ethnicity*. Manchester: Greater Manchester Combined Authority.

Goldade K (2011) Babies and belonging: Reproduction, citizenship, and undocumented Nicaraguan labor migrant women in Costa Rica. *Medical Anthropology* 30(5): 545–568.

Gov.uk (n.d.-a) *Asylum support: What you'll get.* Available at: https://www.gov.uk/asylum-support/what-youll-get (accessed 9 June 2024).

Gov.uk (n.d.-b) *Family visas: Apply, extend or switch.* Available at: https://www.gov.uk/uk-family-visa (accessed 30 April 2024).

Gov.uk (n.d.-c) *Pay for UK healthcare as part of your immigration application.* Available at: https://www.gov.uk/healthcare-immigration-application/how-much-pay (accessed 3 June 2024).

Gov.uk (n.d.-d) *Visit the UK as a standard visitor.* Available at: https://www.gov.uk/standard-visitor (accessed 5 May 2024).

Gov.uk (2021) *Universal Credit: Support for a maximum of 2 children: Information for claimaints.* Available at: https://www.gov.uk/guidance/universal-credit-and-families-with-more-than-2-children-information-for-claimants (accessed 30 May 2024).

Gower M, McKinney C, and Meade L (2022) Asylum seekers: the permission to work policy. London: House of Commons Library.

Grayson J (2018) Rodents, bedbugs, mould: UK asylum housing still a hostile environment. *Open Democracy.* Available at: https://www.opendemocracy.net/en/shine-a-light/rodents-bedbugs-mould-uk-asylum-housing-hostile-environment/ (accessed 27 January 2025).

Greengross P, Grant K, and Collini E (1999) *The History and Development of the UK National Health Service 1948 - 1999.* London: DFID Health System Resource Centre.

Gromada A and Richardson D (2021) *Where do rich countries stand on childcare?* Florence: UNICEF Office of Research–Innocenti.

Hall SM (2023) Social reproduction, labour and austerity: Carrying the future. *The Sociological Review* 71(1): 27–46.

Ham C (2023) *The Rise and Decline of the NHS in England 2000–20. How Political Failure Led to the Crisis in the NHS and Social Care.* London: The King's Fund.

Henderson J, Gao H, and Redshaw M (2013) Experiencing maternity care: the care received and perceptions of women from different ethnic groups. *BMC Pregnancy and Childbirth* 13: 1–14.

Heslehurst N, Brown H, Pemu A, Coleman H, and Rankin J (2018) Perinatal health outcomes and care among asylum seekers and refugees: a systematic review of systematic reviews. *BMC Medicine* 16: 1–25.

Higginbottom GMA, Evans C, Morgan M, Bharj KK, Eldridge J, and Hussain B (2019) Experience of and access to maternity care in the UK by immigrant women: a narrative synthesis systematic review. *BMJ Open* 9(12): e029478.

HL Deb (16 March 2015) *vol. 760, col. 908*. Available at: https://hansard.parliament.uk/Lords/2015-03-16/debates/bee44526-5526-49bf-84f0-d7ab541d3050/LordsChamber#contribution-1503166000040 (accessed 10 February 2025).

Hoberman J (2012) *Black and Blue: The Origins and Consequences of Medical Racism*. Berkeley; Los Angeles; London: University of California Press.

Holston J (1999) Spaces of insurgent citizenship. In: Holston J (ed) *Cities and Citizenship*. Durham, NC; London: Duke University Press, pp 155–174.

Home Office (2002) *Secure Borders, Safe Haven – Integration with Diversity in Modern Britain*. London: The Stationery Office.

Home Office (2006) *A Points-Based System: Making Migration Work for Britain*. London: The Stationery Office.

Home Office (2012) *Statement of Intent: Family Migration*. London: Home Office Publications.

Home Office (2013a) *Controlling immigration – regulating migrant access to health services in the UK. Consultation document*. London: Home Office.

Home Office (2013b) *Controlling immigration – regulating migrant access to health services in the UK. Results of the public consultation*. London: Home Office.

Home Office (2014) *Public funds*. Available at: https://www.gov.uk/government/uploads/system/uploads/attachment_data/file/284160/Public_funds_v12_0EXT.pdf (accessed 15 June 2014).

Home Office (2023) *Paying an NHS debt*. Available at: https://www.gov.uk/guidance/paying-an-nhs-debt (accessed 17 February 2024).

Home Office (2024) *Migrant Victims of Domestic Abuse Concession (formerly the destitute domestic violence concession [DDVC])*. London: Home Office.

Home Office and Department of Health (2017) *Memorandum of understanding between Health and Social Care Information Centre and the Home Office and the Department of Health*. London: Department of Health and Social Care; Home Office.

Hooberman L, Howell FM, Keegan R, and Rubin LR (2023) 'Not that it makes you less of a mother, but...': Navigating discourses of responsible motherhood in the context of VBAC. *Feminism & Psychology* 33(4): 569–588.

Horn A (2023) Birthing while black. *Red Pepper*. Available at: https://www.redpepper.org.uk/society/race-racism/birthing-while-black-pregnancy-bodies-nhs-childbirth-maternity-medical-racism-carcerality/ (accessed 27 January 2025).

Hughes SM (2020) On resistance in human geography. *Progress in Human Geography* 44(6): 1141–1160.

Hughes SM, Murrey A, Krishnan S, van Teijlingen K, Daley PO, Nowicki M, et al (2022) Interventions in the political geographies of resistance: The contributions of Cindi Katz, 15 years on. *Political Geography* 97: 102666.

Humphris R (2017) Borders of home: Roma migrant mothers negotiating boundaries in home encounters. *Journal of Ethnic and Migration Studies* 43(7): 1190–1204.

Hynes P (2011) *The Dispersal and Social Exclusion of Asylum Seekers: Between Liminality and Belonging.* Bristol: Policy Press.

Isin EF (2002) City, democracy and citizenship: Historical images, contemporary practices. In: Isin EF and Turner BS (eds) *Handbook of Citizenship Studies.* London: Sage, pp 305–316.

Jauho M and Helén I (2023) Citizenship by vitality: rethinking the concept of health citizenship. *Distinktion: Journal of Social Theory* 24(3): 467–487.

Jayaweera H and Quigley MA (2010) Health status, health behaviour and healthcare use among migrants in the UK: evidence from mothers in the Millennium Cohort Study. *Social Science & Medicine* 71(5): 1002–1010.

Jensen T (2012) Tough love in tough times. *Studies in the Maternal,* 4(2): 1–26.

Johns M (2020) *10 years of austerity: Eroding resilience in the North of England.* Manchester; Newcastle: Institute for Public Policy Research North.

Joint Council for the Welfare of Immigrants (2017) *Passport Please: The Impact of the Right to Rent Checks on Migrants and Ethnic Minorities in England.* London: Joint Council for the Welfare of Immigrants.

Jomeen J and Redshaw M (2013) Ethnic minority women's experience of maternity services in England. *Ethnicity & Health* 18(3): 280–296.

Jones H (1994) *Health and Society in Twentieth-Century Britain.* Harlow; New York: Longman Group.

Jones H, Gunaratnam Y, Bhattacharyya G, Davies W, Dhaliwal S, Forkert K, et al (2017) *Go Home?: The Politics of Immigration Controversies.* Manchester: Manchester University Press.

Jorgensen N (2024) *Family fortunes: The UK's new income requirement for partner visas.* Available at: https://migrationobservatory.ox.ac.uk/resources/comme ntaries/family-fortunes-the-uks-new-income-requirement-for-partner-visas/ (accessed 5 May 2024).

Katz C (2004) *Growing Up Global: Economic Restructuring and Children's Everyday Lives.* Minneapolis, MN: University of Minnesota Press.

Kennedy P and Kodate N (2015) *Maternity Services and Policy in an International Context: Risk, Citizenship and Welfare Regimes.* Abingdon, Oxon; New York: Routledge.

Khan K (2022) The securitisation of language borders and the (re) production of inequalities. *Tesol Quarterly* 56(4): 1458–1470.

Kirkup J and Winnett R (2012) Theresa May interview: 'We're going to give illegal migrants a really hostile reception'. *The Telegraph Online.* Available at: https://www.telegraph.co.uk/news/0/theresa-may-interview-going-give-illegal-migrants-really-hostile/ (accessed 27 January 2025).

Kivelä S and Moisio S (2017) The state as a space of health: On the geopolitics and biopolitics of health-care systems. *Territory, Politics, Governance* 5(1): 28–46.

Klein R (2013) *The New Politics of the NHS: From Creation to Reinvention.* Oxford; New York: Radcliffe Publishing.

Klug F (1989) 'Oh to be in England': The British case study. In: Yuval-Davis N and Anthias F (eds) *Woman-Nation-State.* Basingstoke: Palgrave MacMillan, pp 16–35.

Knight M and Bevan C (2021) Achieving safer maternity care in the UK. *BMJ* 372.

Knight M and Stanford S (2022) Ockenden: another shocking review of maternity services. *BMJ* 377.

Knight M, Bunch K, Felker A, Patel R, Kotnis R, Kenyon S, et al (2023) *Saving Lives, Improving Mothers' Care: Lessons Learned to Inform Maternity Care from the UK and Ireland Confidential Enquiries into Maternal Deaths and Morbidity 2019–21.* Oxford: National Perinatal Epidemiology Unit, University of Oxford.

Knight M, Bunch K, Tufnell D, Shakespeare J, Kotnis R, Kenyon S, et al (2019) *Saving Lives, Improving Mothers' Care: Lessons Learned to Inform Maternity Care from the UK and Ireland Confidential Enquiries into Maternal Deaths and Morbidity 2015–17.* Oxford: National Perinatal Epidemiology Unit, University of Oxford.

Kofman E (2004) Gendered global migrations: diversity and stratification. *International Feminist Journal of Politics* 6(4): 643–665.

Krachler N and Greer I (2015) When does marketisation lead to privatisation? Profit-making in English health services after the 2012 Health and Social Care Act. *Social Science & Medicine* 124: 215–223.

Kundnani A (2014) *The Muslims are Coming!: Islamophobia, Extremism, and the Domestic War on Terror.* London: Verso Books.

Lafond S (2015) *Current NHS Spending in England.* London: The Health Foundation.

Larios L (2023) Precarious reproductive citizenship: gaps in employment protections for pregnant precarious status migrants in Canada. *Citizenship Studies* 27(1): 19–37.

Laslett B and Brenner J (1989) Gender and social reproduction: historical perspectives. *Sociological Forum* 14(1): 381–404.

Lazarus ES (1994) What do women want?: Issues of choice, control, and class in pregnancy and childbirth. *Medical Anthropology Quarterly* 8(1): 25–46.

Lister R (2003) *Citizenship: Feminist Perspectives.* Basingstoke, Hampshire: Palgrave Macmillan.

Lo Iacono V, Symonds P, and Brown DH (2016) Skype as a tool for qualitative research interviews. *Sociological Research Online* 21(2): 103–117.

Lonergan G (2012) Reproductive justice and migrant women in Great Britain. *Women: A Cultural Review* 23(1): 26–45.

Lonergan G (2015) Migrant women and social reproduction under austerity. *Feminist Review* 109(1): 124–145.

Lonergan G (2018) Reproducing the 'national home': gendering domopolitics. *Citizenship Studies* 22(1): 1–18.

Lonergan G (2024a) Pregnant racialised migrants and the ubiquitous border: the hostile environment as a technology of stratified reproduction. *Critical Social Policy* 44(2): 222–241.

Lonergan G (2024b) Reproduction and the expanding border: Pregnant migrants as a 'problem' in the 2014 Immigration Act. *Sociology* 58(1): 140–157.

Lowe P (2016) *Reproductive Health and Maternal Sacrifice: Women, Choice and Responsibility*. London: Palgrave MacMillan.

Luibhéid E (2013) *Pregnant on Arrival: Making the Illegal Immigrant*. Minneapolis: University of Minnesota Press.

Lupton D (2012) *Medicine as Culture: Illness, Disease and the Body* (3rd edn). London: SAGE Publications.

Mahler SJ and Pessar PR (2006) Gender matters: Ethnographers bring gender from the periphery toward the core of migration studies. *International Migration Review* 40(1): 27–63.

Malacrida C and Boulton T (2014) The best laid plans? Women's choices, expectations and experiences in childbirth. *Health* 18(1): 41–59.

Malakasis C and Sahraoui N (2020) Introducing gender into the theorization of health-related (un)deservingness: Ethnographic insights from Athens and Melilla. In: Sahraoui N (ed) *Borders Across Healthcare: Moral Economies of Healthcare and Migration in Europe*. New York; Oxford: Berghahn Books.

Mamo L and Alston-Stepnitz E (2015) Queer intimacies and structural inequalities: New directions in stratified reproduction. *Journal of Family Issues* 36(4): 519–540.

Marmot M, Allen J, Boyce T, Goldblatt P, and Morrison, J (2020) *Health equity in England: The Marmot Review 10 years on*. London: The Health Foundation.

Marshall TH (1950/2009) Citizenship and social class. In: Manza J and Sauder M (eds) *Inequality and Society*. New York: W.W. Norton & Co., pp 148–154.

McClintock A (1995) *Imperial Leather: Race, Gender, and Sexuality in the Colonial Contest*. New York; Abingdon, Oxon: Routledge.

McIntosh T (2012) *A Social History of Maternity and Childbirth: Key Themes in Maternity Care*. Abingdon, Oxon; New York: Routledge.

McPhail D, Bombak A, Ward P, and Allison J (2016) Wombs at risk, wombs as risk: Fat women's experiences of reproductive care. *Fat Studies* 5(2): 98–115.

Medien K (2021) NHS Apartheid: On resisting NHS charges for overseas visitor healthcare. *Discover Society* 1(4).

Medien K (2023) No pass laws here! Internal border controls and the global 'hostile environment'. *Sociology* 57(4): 940–956.

Mezzadra S and Neilson B (2013) *Border as Method, or the Multiplication of Labour*. Durham, NC; London: Duke University Press.

Mold A (2010) Patient groups and the construction of the patient-consumer in Britain: An historical overview. *Journal of Social Policy* 39(4): 505–521.

Mondon A and Winter A (2020) *Reactionary Democracy: How Racism and the Populist Far Right Became Mainstream*. London; New York: Verso Books.

Moniz MH, Spector-Bagdady K, Perritt JB, Heisler M, Loder CM, Wetmore MK, et al (2022) Balancing enhanced contraceptive access with risk of reproductive injustice: A United States comparative case study. *Contraception* 113: 88–94.

Montalmant KE and Ettinger AK (2024) The racial disparities in maternal mortality and impact of structural racism and implicit racial bias on pregnant Black women: a review of the literature. *Journal of Racial and Ethnic Health Disparities* 11(6): 3658–3677.

Morris M and Nanda S (2021) *Towards True Universal Care: Reforming the NHS Charging System*. London: Institute for Public Policy Research.

National Maternity Review (2016) *Better Births: Improving Outcomes of Maternity Services in England*. London: NHS England.

Nellums LB, Powis J, Jones L, Miller A, Rustage K, Russell N, et al (2021) 'It's a life you're playing with': A qualitative study on experiences of NHS maternity services among undocumented migrant women in England. *Social Science & Medicine* 270: 113610.

Nestel S (1994) 'Other' mothers: race and representation in natural childbirth discourse. *Resources for Feminist Research* 23(4): 5.

NHS (n.d.) *Your pregnancy care*. Available at: https://www.nhs.uk/pregnancy/your-pregnancy-care/ (accessed 3 June 2024).

NHS (2024) *Where to give birth: the options*. Available at: https://www.nhs.uk/pregnancy/labour-and-birth/preparing-for-the-birth/where-to-give-birth-the-options/ (accessed 3 June 2024).

NHS England (2024) *NHS Data Model and Dictionary*. Available at: https://www.datadictionary.nhs.uk/nhs_business_definitions/nhs_trust.html (accessed 3 June 2024).

NRPF Network (n.d.) *Social services support for families*. Available at: https://www.nrpfnetwork.org.uk/information-and-resources/rights-and-entitlements/support-options-for-people-with-nrpf/social-services-support-for-families/when-will-a-family-be-eligible#guide-content (accessed 9 June 2024).

Nyers P (2004) Introduction: What's left of citizenship? *Citizenship Studies* 8(3): 203–215.

Oakley A (2016) The sociology of childbirth: an autobiographical journey through four decades of research. *Sociology of Health & Illness* 38(5): 689–705.

Obionu IM, Onyedinma CA, Mielewczyk F, and Boyle E (2023) UK maternity care experiences of ethnic minority and migrant women: Systematic review. *Public Health Nursing* 40(6): 846–856.

Office for National Statistics (2023a) *How Life has Changed in Kirklees: Census 2021.* Available at: https://www.ons.gov.uk/visualisations/censusareachanges/E08000034/ (accessed 29 May 2024).

Office for National Statistics (2023b) *How Life has Changed in Leeds: Census 2021.* Available at: https://www.ons.gov.uk/visualisations/censusareachanges/E08000035/ (accessed 29 May 2024).

Office for National Statistics (2023c) *How Life has Changed in Manchester: Census 2021.* Available at: https://www.ons.gov.uk/visualisations/censusareachanges/E08000003/ (accessed 29 May 2024).

Olafsdottir S and Bakhtiari E (2015) Citizenship and healthcare policy. In: Kuhlmann E, Blank RH, Bourgeault IL, and Wendt C (eds) *The Palgrave International Handbook of Healthcare Policy and Governance.* Basingstoke; New York: Palgrave Macmillan, pp 561–577.

Paasi A (1999) Boundaries as social practice and discourse: The Finnish-Russian border. *Regional Studies* 33(7): 669–680.

Pařízková A, Clausen JA, Balaam M-C, Haith-Cooper M, Roosalu T, Migliorini L, et al (2024) Inclusiveness of access policies to maternity care for migrant women across Europe: A policy review. *Maternal and Child Health Journal* 28(3): 470–480.

Parliament. House of Commons (1980) *Perinatal and neonatal mortality. Second report from the Social Services Committee (HC 1979–1980; 663).* London: House of Commons.

Parliament. House of Commons (2013) *Public Bill Committee Proceedings. Immigration Bill.* London: House of Commons.

Parreñas RS (2014) The intimate labour of transnational communication. *Families, Relationships and Societies* 3(3): 425.

Pateman C (1989) *The Disorder of Women.* Cambridge: Polity Press.

Pateman C (1992) Equality, difference, subordination: the politics of motherhood and women's citizenship. In: Bock G and James S (eds) *Beyond Equality and Difference.* London: Routledge, pp 14–27.

Pedersen GS, Grøntved A, Mortensen LH, Andersen A-MN, and Rich-Edwards J (2014) Maternal mortality among migrants in Western Europe: a meta-analysis. *Maternal and Child Health Journal* 18: 1628–1638.

Pellander S (2021) Buy me love: Entanglements of citizenship, income and emotions in regulating marriage migration. *Journal of Ethnic and Migration Studies* 47(2): 464–479.

Peter M, Wheeler R, Awe T, and Abe C (2022) *The Black Maternity Experiences Survey: A Nationwide Study of Black Women's Experiences of Maternity Services in the United Kingdom*. London: FiveXMore.

Peterson VS (2020) Family matters in racial logics: Tracing intimacies, inequalities, and ideologies. *Review of International Studies* 46(2): 177–196.

Phillimore J (2015) Delivering maternity services in an era of superdiversity: The challenges of novelty and newness. *Ethnic and Racial Studies* 38(4): 568–582.

Phillimore J (2016) Migrant maternity in an era of superdiversity: New migrants' access to, and experience of, antenatal care in the West Midlands, UK. *Social Science & Medicine* 148: 152–159.

Pickles C (2019) Leaving women behind: The application of evidence-based guidelines, law, and obstetric violence by omission. In: Pickles C and Herring J (eds) *Childbirth, Vulnerability and Law*. Routledge, pp 140–160.

Pollock AM (2005) *NHS plc: The Privatisation of Our Health Care*. London; New York: Verso Books.

Porter D (2011) *Health Citizenship: Essays in Social Medicine and Biomedical Politics*. Berkeley; Los Angeles; London: University of California Press.

Purcell M (2003) Citizenship and the right to the global city: Reimagining the capitalist world order. *International Journal of Urban and Regional Research* 27(3): 564–590.

Raghuram P (2004) Crossing borders: Gender and migration. In: Staeheli LA, Kofman E, and Peake LJ (eds) *Mapping Women, Making Politics: Feminist Perspectives on Political Geography*. New York; Abingdon, Oxon: Routledge, pp 185–197.

Ray JG, Park AL, Dzakpasu S, Dayan N, Deb-Rinker P, Luo W, et al (2018) Prevalence of severe maternal morbidity and factors associated with maternal mortality in Ontario, Canada. *JAMA Network Open* 1(7): e184571–e184571.

Reis S and Stephens L (2022) *Spring Budget 2022: Childcare and gender*. London: Women's Budget Group.

Rich M (2016) The curse of civilised woman: Race, gender and the pain of childbirth in nineteenth-century American medicine. *Gender & History* 28(1): 57–76.

Richardson EH and Turner BS (2001) Sexual, intimate or reproductive citizenship? *Citizenship Studies* 5(3): 329–338.

Rier DA (2022) Responsibility in medical sociology: A second, reflexive look. *The American Sociologist* 53(4): 663–684.

Riley NE and Chatterjee N (2023) *Controlling Reproduction: Women, Society, and State Power*. Cambridge; Hoboken, NJ: Polity Press.

Roberts DE (2017) *Killing the Black Body: Race, Reproduction, and the Meaning of Liberty*. New York: Vintage Books/Random House.

Rodrigues J (2015) Clause Four at 20: Tony Blair changes the Labour party constitution. *The Guardian Online.* Available at: https://www.theguardian.com/politics/from-the-archive-blog/2015/apr/29/clause-four-labour-party-tony-blair-20-1995 (accessed 27 January 2025).

Rose N (1999) *Powers of Freedom: Reframing Political Thought.* Cambridge; New York; Port Melbourne; Madrid; Cape Town: Cambridge University Press.

Roseneil S, Crowhurst I, Hellesund T, Santos AC, and Stoilova M (2020) *The Tenacity of the Couple-norm: Intimate Citizenship Regimes in a Changing Europe.* London: UCL Press.

Roseneil S, Crowhurst I, Santos AC, and Stoilova M (2013) Reproduction and citizenship/reproducing citizens: Editorial introduction. *Citizenship Studies* 17(8): 901–911.

Ross L, Derkas E, Peoples W, and Bridgewater Toure P (eds) (2017) *Radical Reproductive Justice: Foundation, Theory, Practice, Critique.* New York: Feminist Press at CUNY.

Ross LJ (2006) The color of choice: White supremacy and reproductive justice. In: Incite! Women of Color Against Violence (ed) *Color of Violence: The INCITE! Anthology.* Cambridge, MA: South End Press, pp 53–65.

Rowland D (2023) How private finance is crippling health and social care. *British Politics and Policy at LSE.* Available at: https://blogs.lse.ac.uk/politicsandpolicy/how-private-finance-is-crippling-health-and-social-care/ (accessed 27 January 2025).

Rowntree M (2024) Hear me. *Midwives: The Official Journal of the Royal College of Midwives* 27: 49–53.

Royal College of Obstetricians and Gynaecologists (n.d.) *RCOG Position Statement: Equitable access to maternity care for refugee, asylum seeking and undocumented migrant women.* Available at: https://www.rcog.org.uk/about-us/campaigning-and-opinions/position-statements/position-statement-equitable-access-to-maternity-care-for-refugee-asylum-seeking-and-undocumented-migrant-women/ (accessed 18 June 2024).

Royal College of Midwives (2021a) *Caring for Vulnerable Migrant Women.* London: The Royal College of Midwives.

Royal College of Midwives (2021b) *Improving Maternity: Learning from Reviews of Maternity Services.* London: The Royal College of Midwives.

Royal College of Midwives (2022a) *Position Statement: Safe Staffing.* London: The Royal College of Midwives.

Royal College of Midwives (2022b) *RCM calls for end to migrant women maternity charging over safety fears.* Available at: https://www.rcm.org.uk/media-releases/2022/february/rcm-calls-for-end-to-migrant-women-maternity-charging-over-safety-fears/ (accessed 21 June 2024).

Runnymede Trust (2000) *The Future of Multi-ethnic Britain: The Parekh Report.* London: Profile Books.

Sahraoui N (2020a) *Borders Across Healthcare: Moral Economies of Healthcare and Migration in Europe*. New York; Oxford: Berghahn Books.

Sahraoui N (2020b) Gendering the care/control nexus of the humanitarian border: Women's bodies and gendered control of mobility in a EUropean borderland. *Environment and Planning D: Society and Space* 38(5): 905–922.

Sahraoui N (2021) Constructions of undeservingness around the figure of the undocumented pregnant woman in the French department of Mayotte. *Social Policy and Society* 20(3): 475–486.

Samantrai R (2002) *AlterNatives: Black Feminism in the Postimperial Nation*. Stanford: Stanford University Press.

Sassoon AS (1987) Women's new social role. In: Sassoon AS (ed) *Women and the State*. London: Hutchinson, pp 158–188.

Schrecker T and Bambra C (2015) *How Politics Makes Us Sick: Neoliberal Epidemics*. Springer.

Shan H, Saharso S, van Kroonenburg N, and Henrichs J (2023) Understanding the relationship between maternity care providers and middle-class Chinese migrant women in the Netherlands: A qualitative study. *Midwifery* 125: 103775.

Shim JK (2010) Cultural health capital: a theoretical approach to understanding health care interactions and the dynamics of unequal treatment. *Journal of Health and Social Behavior* 51(1): 1–15.

Shortall C, McMorran J, Taylor K, Traianou A, Garcia de Frutos M, Jones L, et al (2015) *Experiences of Pregnant Migrant Women Receiving Ante/Peri and Postnatal Care in the UK: A Longitudinal Follow-up Study of Doctors of the World's London Drop-in Clinic Attendees*. London: Doctors of the World.

Siddiqui S (2021) Racing the nation: towards a theory of reproductive racism. *Race & Class* 63(2): 3–20.

Sirriyeh A (2015) 'All you need is love and £18,600': Class and the new UK family migration rules. *Critical Social Policy* 35(2): 228–247.

Sister Song (n.d.) *Reproductive justice*. Available at: https://www.sistersong.net/reproductive-justice/ (accessed 4 March 2024).

Small R, Roth C, Raval M, Shafiei T, Korfker D, Heaman M, et al (2014) Immigrant and non-immigrant women's experiences of maternity care: A systematic and comparative review of studies in five countries. *BMC Pregnancy and Childbirth* 14: 1–17.

Small S and Solomos J (2006) Race, immigration and politics in Britain: Changing policy agendas and conceptual paradigms 1940s–2000s. *International Journal of Comparative Sociology* 47(3–4): 235–257.

Smietana M, Thompson C and Twine FW (2018) Making and breaking families—reading queer reproductions, stratified reproduction and reproductive justice together. *Reproductive Biomedicine & Society Online* 7: 112.

Solazzo AL (2019) Different and not equal: The uneven association of race, poverty, and abortion laws on abortion timing. *Social Problems* 66(4): 519–547.

Solinger R (2001) *Beggars and Choosers: How the Politics of Choice Shapes Adoption, Abortion, and Welfare in the United States*. New York: Hill and Wang.

Solomos J (2003) *Race and Racism in Britain*. Basingstoke, Hampshire: Palgrave MacMillan.

Sowemimo A (2023) *Divided: Racism, Medicine and Why We Need to Decolonise Healthcare*. London: Profile Books.

Soysal YN (2012) Citizenship, immigration, and the European social project: Rights and obligations of individuality. *British Journal of Sociology* 63(1): 1–21.

Spillers HJ (2022) Mama's baby, papa's maybe: An American grammar book. *Diacritics* 17(2): 64–81.

Spratt TJR (2022) Reconceptualising Judith Butler's theory of 'grievability' in relation to the UK's 'war on obesity': Personal responsibility, biopolitics and disposability. *The Sociological Review* 70(3): 474–488.

Springsteen B (1984) *Born in the USA*. New York: Columbia Records.

Strasser E, Kraler A, Bonjour S, and Bilger V (2009) Doing family: Responses to the constructions of 'the migrant family' across Europe. *The History of the Family* 14(2): 165–176.

Sturges JE and Hanrahan KJ (2004) Comparing telephone and face-to-face qualitative interviewing: A research note. *Qualitative Research* 4(1): 107–118.

Sudhinaraset M, Kolodner RA, and Nakphong MK (2023) Maternity care at the intersections of language, ethnicity, and immigration status: a qualitative study. *Women's Health Issues* 33(6): 618–625.

Thane P (1996) *The Foundations of the Welfare State*. Abingdon, Oxon; New York: Routledge.

The Health Foundation (2024a) *District health authorities (DHAs)*. Available at: https://navigator.health.org.uk/theme/district-health-authorities-dhas# (accessed 3 June 2024).

The Health Foundation (2024b) *Health Act 1999*. Available at: https://navigator.health.org.uk/theme/health-act-1999 (accessed 3 June 2024).

The Health Foundation (2024c) *Private Finance Initiative (PFI) schemes*. Available at: https://navigator.health.org.uk/theme/private-finance-initiative-pfi-schemes (accessed 02 June 2024).

The Health Foundation (2024d) *Structural changes from Health and Social Care Act (2012)*. Available at: https://navigator.health.org.uk/theme/structural-changes-health-and-social-care-act-2012 (accessed 3 June 2024).

The King's Fund (2021) *Is the NHS being privatised?* Available at: https://www.kingsfund.org.uk/insight-and-analysis/long-reads/big-election-questions-nhs-privatised (accessed 20 March 2024).

The King's Fund (2023) *The NHS budget and how it has changed*. Available at: https://www.kingsfund.org.uk/insight-and-analysis/data-and-charts/nhs-budget-nutshell (accessed 19 March 2024).

Torjesen I (2021) NICE backtracks on advice to induce labour at 39 weeks in ethnic minority women. *The BMJ* 375.

Treichler PA (1990) Feminism, medicine, and the meaning of childbirth. In: Jacobus M, Fox Keller E, and Shuttleworth S (eds) *Body/Politics: Women and the Discourses of Science*. New York; London: Routledge, pp 113–138.

Turner BS (2008) Citizenship, reproduction and the state: International marriage and human rights. *Citizenship Studies* 12(1): 45–54.

Turner J (2015) The family migration visa in the history of marriage restrictions: Postcolonial relations and the UK border. *The British Journal of Politics and International Relations* 17(4): 623–643.

Turner J (2017) Domesticating the 'troubled family': Racialised sexuality and the postcolonial governance of family life in the UK. *Environment and Planning D: Society and Space* 35(5): 933–950.

Turner J (2020) *Bordering Intimacy: Postcolonial Governance and the Policing of Family*. Manchester: Manchester University Press.

Tyler I (2008) 'Chav mum chav scum': Class disgust in contemporary Britain. *Feminist Media Studies* 8(1): 17–34.

Tyler I (2010) Designed to fail: a biopolitics of British citizenship. *Citizenship Studies* 14(1): 61–74.

Tyler I (2013) *Revolting Subjects: Social Abjection and Resistance in Neoliberal Britain*. London; New York: Zed Books.

UK Visas and Immigration (2024) *Guidance: UK visa requirements (accessible version)*. Available at: https://www.gov.uk/government/publications/uk-visa-requirements-list-for-carriers/uk-visa-requirements-for-internatio nal-carriers (accessed 3 May 2024).

van der Waal R, Mayra K, Horn A, and Chadwick R (2023) Obstetric violence: An intersectional refraction through abolition feminism. *Feminist Anthropology* 4(1): 91–114.

van Houdt F, Suvarierol S, and Schinkel W (2011) Neoliberal communitarian citizenship: Current trends toward 'earned citizenship' in the United Kingdom, France and the Netherlands. *International Sociology* 26(3): 408–432.

Vohra A (2023) Italy now has conspiracy theory as national policy. *Foreign Policy*. Available at: https://foreignpolicy.com/2023/05/08/italy-mel oni-great-replacement-conspiracy-theory-immigration/ (accessed 27 January 2025).

Waddan A (2018) Is health care in England really on the road to privatization? *Political Science Quarterly* 133(4): 669–695.

Walker C and Farrington R (2021) Charging for NHS care and its impact on maternal health. *British Journal of General Practice* 71(705): 155–156.

Werbner P and Yuval-Davis N (1999) Chapter 1: Introduction. Women and the new discourse of citizenship. In: Yuval-Davis N and Werbner P (eds) *Women, Citizenship and Difference*. London; New York: Zed Books, pp 1–38.

Willen S (2012) Migration, 'illegality', and health: Mapping embodied vulnerability and debating health-related deservingness. *Social Science & Medicine* (74): 805–811.

Willen SS and Cook J (2016) Health-related deservingness. In: Thomas F (ed) *Handbook of Migration and Health*. Cheltenham, UK; Northampton, MA: Edward Elgar Publishing, pp 95–118.

World Health Organization (2015) *The Prevention and Elimination of Disrespect and Abuse During Facility-based Childbirth*. Geneva: World Health Organization.

Worley C (2005) 'It's not about race. It's about the community': New Labour and 'community cohesion'. *Critical Social Policy* 25(4): 483–496.

Wray H (2011) *Regulating Marriage Migration into the UK: A Stranger in the Home*. Farnham, Surrey; Burlington, VT: Routledge.

Wu J, Braunschweig Y, Harris LH, Horner-Johnson W, Ernst SD, and Stevens B (2019) Looking back while moving forward: A justice-based, intersectional approach to research on contraception and disability. *Contraception* 99(5): 267–271.

Yorkshire and Humberside Maternity Stream (2024) *Yorkshire and Humberside Maternity Stream*. Available at: https://maternity-yh.cityofsanctuary.org/ (accessed 29 May 2024).

Yuval-Davis N (1997) *Gender and Nation*. London; Thousand Oaks, CA; New Delhi: Sage Publications.

Yuval-Davis N, Anthias F, and Kofman E (2005) Secure borders and safe haven and the gendered politics of belonging: Beyond social cohesion. *Ethnic and Racial Studies* 28(3): 513–535.

Yuval-Davis N, Wemyss G, and Cassidy K (2018) Everyday bordering, belonging and the reorientation of British immigration legislation. *Sociology* 52(2): 228–244.

Yuval-Davis N, Wemyss G, and Cassidy K (2019) *Bordering*. Cambridge; Medford, MA: Polity Press.

Zhu C (2023) Barriers and challenges of immigrant women's access to and experience of optimal maternity care. *The Columbia University Journal of Global Health* 13(1).

Zwart JJ, Jonkers MD, Richters A, Ory F, Bloemenkamp KW, Duvekot JJ, et al (2011) Ethnic disparity in severe acute maternal morbidity: a nationwide cohort study in the Netherlands. *European Journal of Public Health* 21(2): 229–234.

Index